Evoking Through Design

Contemporary Moods in Architecture

Guest-Edited by
MATIAS DEL CAMPO

Profile
No 244

ARCHITECTURAL DESIGN
November/December 2016

ISSN 0003-8504
ISBN 978-1119-099581

Editorial Offices
John Wiley & Sons
9600 Garsington Road
Oxford
OX4 2DQ

T +44 (0)1865 776868

Consultant Editor
Helen Castle

Managing Editor
Caroline Ellerby
Caroline Ellerby Publishing

Freelance Contributing Editor
Abigail Grater

Publisher
Paul Sayer

Art Direction + Design
CHK Design:
Christian Küsters
Christos Kontogeorgos

Production Editor
Elizabeth Gongde

Prepress
Artmedia, London

Printed in Italy by Printer
Trento Srl

Journal Customer Services
For ordering information,
claims and any enquiry
concerning your journal
subscription please go to
www.wileycustomerhelp
.com/ask or contact your
nearest office.

Americas
E: cs-journals@wiley.com
T: +1 781 388 8598 or
+1 800 835 6770 (toll free
in the USA & Canada)

**Europe, Middle East
and Africa**
E: cs-journals@wiley.com
T: +44 (0)1865 778315

Asia Pacific
E: cs-journals@wiley.com
T: +65 6511 8000

Japan (for Japanese-
speaking support)
E: cs-japan@wiley.com
T: +65 6511 8010 or 005 316
50 480 (toll-free)

Visit our Online Customer
Help available in 7 languages
at www.wileycustomerhelp
.com/ask

Print ISSN: 0003-8504
Online ISSN: 1554-2769

Prices are for six issues
and include postage and
handling charges. Individual-
rate subscriptions must be
paid by personal cheque or
credit card. Individual-rate
subscriptions may not be
resold or used as library
copies.

All prices are subject to
change without notice.

Identification Statement
Periodicals Postage paid
at Rahway, NJ 07065.
Air freight and mailing in
the USA by Mercury Media
Processing, 1850 Elizabeth
Avenue, Suite C, Rahway,
NJ 07065, USA.

USA Postmaster
Please send address changes
to *Architectural Design*,
John Wiley & Sons Inc.,
c/o The Sheridan Press,
PO Box 465, Hanover,
PA 17331, USA

Rights and Permissions
Requests to the Publisher
should be addressed to:
Permissions Department
John Wiley & Sons Ltd
The Atrium
Southern Gate
Chichester
West Sussex PO19 8SQ
UK

F: +44 (0)1243 770 620
E: Permissions@wiley.com

Subscribe to ⊿
⊿ is published bimonthly
and is available to purchase
on both a subscription basis
and as individual volumes
at the following prices.

Prices
Individual copies:
£24.99 / US$39.95
Individual issues on
⊿ App for iPad:
£9.99 / US$13.99
Mailing fees for print
may apply

Annual Subscription Rates
Student: £84 / US$129
print only
Personal: £128 / US$201
print and iPad access
Institutional: £275 / US$516
print or online
Institutional: £330 / US$620
combined print and online
6-issue subscription on
⊿ App for iPad: £44.99 /
US$64.99

Front and back
cover: Dextro/Walter
Gorgosilits, *K456_64D*,
2015. © Dextro.org

Inside front cover:
Alisa Andrasek with
Wonderlab, XenoCells,
'Exo-Evolution'
exhibition, ZKM|Center
for Art and Media ,
Karlsruhe, 2015. © Alisa
Andrasek, Wonderlab,
UCL Bartlett, Shawn Liu

06/2016

⊿ ARCHITECTURAL DESIGN

November/December 2016

Profile No. 244

Matias del Campo is a registered architect, designer, and Associate Professor of Architecture at the A Alfred Taubman College of Architecture and Urban Planning at the University of Michigan. His obsessive explorations of contemporary moods are fuelled by the opulent repertoire of materialisation in nature together with cutting-edge technologies, as well as form, as a driving force in design at large.

In 2003 he cofounded the architectural practice SPAN in Vienna, together with Sandra Manninger. The practice is best known for its speculative projects dealing with the sophisticated application of contemporary schools of thought in architectural production. Its award-winning projects are particularly informed by Baroque geometries, Romantic sensibilities and continental philosophy, and interrogate the possible contributions of these sensorial and spatial conditions, in combination with the manifold qualities of algorithm-driven methodologies, to the discipline of architecture.

SPAN gained wide recognition for its winning competition entry for the Austrian Pavilion at the 2010 Shanghai World Expo, as well as for the new Brancusi Museum in Paris in 2008. The practice's work was featured at the 2012 Venice Architecture Biennale, at ArchiLab 2013 at the FRAC Centre, Orléans, France, at the 2008 and 2010 Architecture Biennale in Beijing, and in the 2011 solo show 'Formations' at the Museum of Applied Arts (MAK) in Vienna. It is also in the permanent collections of FRAC, MAK, the Albertina museum in Vienna and the Pinakothek der Moderne in Munich. In 2013, SPAN expanded its operations to Shanghai, where the practice is currently working on building projects of varying scales. Design and research awards include the Young-Talent Award for Experimental Tendencies in Architecture (from the Federal Chancellery of Austria), the Rudolph Schindler Scholarship (granted by the Bundesministerium für Unterricht, Kunst und Kultur (BMUKK) and MAK), the Guardian Glass Research Grant and the Accelerate@CERN award.

Del Campo's previous teaching appointments include Visiting Professor at the Dessau Institute of Architecture at the Bauhaus; Guest Professor at the ESARQ School of Architecture in Barcelona; and lecturer at the University of Pennsylvania. He served as Chair of the 'ACADIA 2016: Posthuman Frontiers' conference, and is currently completing his PhD at RMIT University in Melbourne.

Moods
and Other
Ontologic
Catastrop

al
hes

Ensamble Studio,
The Truffle,
Costa da Morte,
Galicia,
Spain,
2010

The Truffle house is part of Ensamble Studio's current series of projects that intentionally negotiate between rough services and clean-shaven planes. Here the raw, deliberately sloppy fringes of the concrete contrasts with the precise cuts executed with a diamond saw and the sober tranquillity of the steel door.

The speculum of speculation is not a thin, flat plate of glass onto which a layer of molten aluminum has been vacuum-sprayed but a funhouse mirror made of hammered metal, whose distortions show us a perversion of a unit's sensibilities.
— Ian Bogost, *Alien Phenomenology, Or What It's Like to Be a Thing*, 2012[1]

Time cools, time clarifies; no mood can be maintained quite unaltered through the course of hours
— Thomas Mann, *Der Zauberberg* (*The Magic Mountain*), 1924[2]

The debate on computational design thinking over the last two decades has focused mainly on techniques, technologies and tools[3] – on how things are done, and not what they do or what they emanate. This has left very little breathing space to contemplate what these computationally driven chunks, pieces, objects and things actually imprint on the world in terms of cultural agency. What traces do they leave? How do they relate to each other, and the rest of the world? How do carved patterns, translucent columns, ultra-black asteroids, massive lacerated blocks and flocks of colourful boulders create an alternative frame for realism?

Instead of perpetuating the techno mantra of computational design, this issue of ⌂ strives to examine the characteristics of contemporary architectural production in terms of their ability to evoke mood, radiate atmospheric conditions and portray phenomenological traits of the sensual as well as the actual. Do these objects de facto have a mood? Is mood part of any possible interrogation? How does it contribute to the study of the nature of being, becoming, existence or reality and the basic categories of being and their relations? 'Mood' and the sublime, it can be argued, have a very close-knit relationship with the nature of aesthetic and artistic experience.

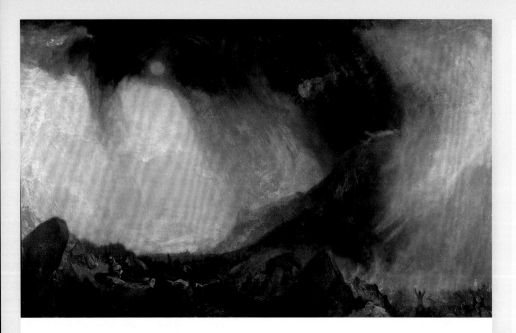

Joseph Mallord
William Turner,
*Snow Storm:
Hannibal and his
Army Crossing the
Alps,*
1812

left: Turner's *Snow
Storm* marks one of the
highlights of what the
German art historian
Heinrich Wölfflin describes
as *'malerisch'* (painterly),
in which the firm contour
of an object is replaced
by a system of relative
light and non-local colour
within the shade, thus
turning shadow, darkness
and luminous effects
into features evoking
atmospheric and moody
conditions.

Stefan Klecheski,
Yingjing Ma and
Siwei Ren,
*Cute Seams,
Seems Cute –
Seagram Building
NYC,*
Taubman College of
Architecture and
Urban Planning,
University of
Michigan,
Ann Arbor,
Michigan,
2016

right: The project occupies
Mies van der Rohe's
Seagram Building and
intentionally perverts the
Miesian form as well as
his material fetishism. In
the process it creates an
uncanny tension between
the well-proportioned
angular properties of the
Seagram Building and the
almost vulgarly bulbous
extensions.

As John McMorrough so eloquently explains in his essay 'Mood Swings: Architectural Affective Disorder' (pp 14–19), mood may at first seem a rather trivial concern upon which to base serious architectural discourse. It sits lightly in the range of behavioural responses (human or not); it has been described as little more than feelings, but no less than a fundamental calibration of the world around us. Mood, it seems, once evoked, provokes. Upon closer examination, however, a whole set of fundamental questions arise concerning the relationship of subject and object, the source of causation, and the universality of responses. In short, a serious study of mood moves quite quickly from something understood as trifling and subject to change (one speaks of a 'shifting mood'), to a fundamental deliberation regarding influence and affect – not primarily as a personal reaction to a particular space, but as a conceptual issue that depicts mood as recurrent and repeatable; that is, transmittable.

The 19th-century German philosopher and notorious misanthrope Arthur Schopenhauer offers a phenomenologically complex account of how we may take aesthetic pleasure in a universe of delightfully weird or massively overwhelming architectural entities. If everything is an object, and achieves will-less contemplation of the ideas that express themselves in these threatening instances, then the objects maintain a 'state of elevation' – a feeling of the sublime.

Where Schopenhauer fails to show some compassion, Benjamin H Bratton makes it a staple of his essay 'Bad Mood: On Design and "Empathy"' (pp 96–101). His examples of buildings worth our emphatic recognition include the vast logistical archipelagos – factories, warehouses, container ships, distribution routes, switching depots – all briefly inhabited by inanimate objects in passing. It could be said that a contemporary moodless architecture already exists, in which those passing objects are incapable of emotion in any normal sense. Yet we build so many houses for them. Perhaps the reasons for this are stranger, more contradictory and more instructive than we realise.

In a Contemporary Mood
The opposite end of the spectrum of considerations is best described by Sylvia Lavin in her 2003 essay 'In a Contemporary Mood',[4] in which she contemplates the contemporary as a speculative terrain triggered by an ambition requiring the identification of a field of architectural effects. These conditions can be understood as being detachable from the logics of causality. One of the primary attributes of the special effects described by Lavin is their inherent ephemeral quality and shelf life. Atmospheric qualities and special effects occupy the same terrain and are intrinsically bounded to the mood of an object. To exemplify this idea, Lavin relies on the Modernist icon Ludwig Mies van der Rohe, an architect strictly bound to the application of effect. The orthogonal anorexic architecture is laced with information by the material effects of glass, marble, bronze and steel.

The only intuitively romantic effect in Mies's work is in the colour of the marble striations, the veining of the Macassar wood, and the merciless reflectivity of the chromed column – ontological dependencies based on material qualities. Contemporary moods operate not on a different but an alternative set of interdependencies far more concerned with the intermediation of aesthetic imprints resulting from a crescendo of temporary material effects. Procedures such as accumulation, lamination, decoration, colouration, agitation, plasticisation and environmentalisation are expressed in an interest in primitive architectural conditions.

The raw, the coarse and also the obscene have a place in this hypogean plane of architectural thinking. Pixels, voxels and cells evoke an alternative universe of atmospheres or moods. François Roche's 'Parrhesia-stases (The Preamble)' (pp 66–71) drags readers deeper into a rabbit-hole called obscenity where they encounter the hidden, the secret and the repulsive as catalysts for condemnation and punishment. Sigmund Freud would certainly have raised an eyebrow, or maybe even two.

It appears that when discussing the properties of mood, the strange is never far away, as also exemplified in the work of Jason Payne and his practice Hirsuta. His Mathilde project, described in his essay on pp 42–5, literally observes a strange and dark object, an asteroid, slowly wobbling and stumbling through our solar system, initiating a new foray into an old subject – object conversation. In a similar vein, in his essay 'The Affects of Realism: Or the Estrangement of the Background' (pp 58–65), Michael Young unfolds some of the historical precedents of defamiliarisation and estrangement, revealing the world to be other than how it is commonly understood to be received. By 'estranging' objects and complicating form, he argues, art as a device has a purpose all of its own and ought to be extended to its fullest.

Young includes such devices as the shifting of narrative points of view (for example, to the nonhuman) and 'the description of an action solely through qualitative sensations, avoiding all direct naming of the action itself. For these formalist critiques, defamiliarisation operates both at the level of inverted conventions (a conceptual project) and heightened attention (a sensation project).' In our own work at SPAN, Sandra Manninger and myself have developed a similar interest in the combination of the conceptual and sensational, which allows interrogation of primordial architectural problems, strange corners, deliquescent walls, flirting ceilings, firm symmetries, adventurous illuminations, a staccato of floors, hairpin columns and sublime naves, and all the intimate relationships between those objects, regardless of its scale. Ore Fashion Stores and Blocks (pp 54–7) are two current projects that address facets of estranged conditions that are familiar yet alien at the same time.

Traditionally in architecture, ambient effects are described as essentially based on material agencies. Indeed, Adolf Loos was able to orchestrate sensations by using the inherent properties of materials. For example, in his American Bar in Vienna (1908), the sensorial reflections active in the room range from the warm grip of the ivory doorknob to the hysterical veining of the marble, and the coldness of the yellow brass and sad endlessness of the implacable mirroring of the ceiling. Loos's play on material effects is thus a vehicle for speculations on defamiliarisation and estrangement.

Along these same lines, Eragatory's '!ntimacy' series of objects attempts to estrange the lineage of the application of 'honest materials' in architecture (see founder Isaie Bloch's article '!ntimacy: Eragatory's Experiments in Materiality, Deep Texture and Mood' on pp 20–25). Although clearly making use of the familiar striations of semiprecious stones such as banded agate or strongly figured onyx, the project wades knee deep into the realms of estrangement, as the undulating weft and colourful layers of these materials are scaled to the size of the impossible. In opposition to the strangeness of the larger-than-life stone banding, Eragatory exploits quasi-common architectural elements to lure us into the safety of familiar spatial conditions. A bathtub, stairs, a pretty lounge chair and remarkably modern glazing emphasise a 'normal' everyday environment, yet hovering above this is the uncanny feeling that an undescribable something is different.

In his article 'Aesthetics as Politics: The Khaleesi Tower on West 57th Street, NYC' (pp 26–33), Mark Foster Gage advocates for the emergence of architecture as a discipline able to articulate itself beyond tamely shaded utilitarian excuses. His New York City tower irritates with no clever intertwining of programme, no cute animalistic metaphors, and no effort to achieve apparent sustainability. Instead it opts to be loved or hated: it gambles with the emotional response, and thus with the mood it evokes. There is certainly a polarity here between the real and the sensual, the object and its qualities.[5]

Messy Things and Raw Figures

The work presented in this issue of ∆ intentionally embraces the coarse and the raw, without ever becoming bucolic. The projects rather play with primordial architectural moments, such as the hut, cave and totem, but express such conditions in a relentlessly contemporary way. It is precisely this romantic desire to explore the archetypical architectural problem (besides huts and caves, findings in contemporary projects deal with colonnades, grottos and facades) that positions the work featured in the issue in an area of architectural production that breaks free from the vicious circle of the postmodern age – avoiding techniques such as collage, ironic referencing of building elements and nostalgia, and instead morphing the primordial into novel conditions that trigger speculations on modes of spatial perception. Examples of this are given in Gilles Retsin's contribution 'Something Else, Something Raw: From ProtoHouse to Blokhut – The Aesthetics of Computational Assemblage' (pp 84–9), where the desire to move away from concrete form and surface is expressed through the use of gruff chunks, cognate pieces and tattered blocks.

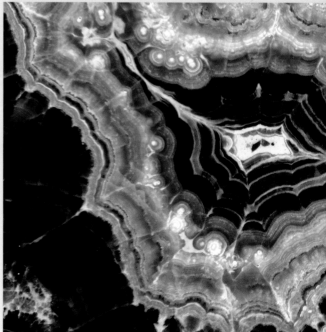

Lucy McRae and
Bart Hess,
Grow on You #2,
2008

Fashion designers by trade,
Lucy McRae and Bart Hess
have developed a mastery
in the combination of the
familiar and the alien. The
project of defamiliarisation
and estrangement reveals
the world to be other
than how it is commonly
understood to be received.
Grow on You #2 literally
negotiates between figure,
object and plane of
observation.

As explained by Mario Carpo in his essay 'Excessive Resolution: From Digital Streamlining to Computational Complexity' (pp 78–83), contemporary computational design is messy. Does it mark a desire for the unexpected, the random, the dirty? The new work presented in this issue enables an alternative, philosophical reframing of narrative and theoretical possibilities. Carpo points towards the notions presented in Graham Harman's *Weird Realism: Lovecraft and Philosophy* (2012),[6] which allow the construction of a speculative frame around architectural projects that to a certain degree deny conventional classification (and thus appear uncanny or weird), but nonetheless contain enough familiar architectural features to be presented as a viable part of the discourse. Apart from the literary description of exotic architectural features, the main strain of Harman's book allows speculation about possible design solutions that are familiar but different, normal but unseen, new and ancient at the same time.

Alisa Andrasek and her Wonderlab colleagues at the Bartlett School of Architecture, University College London (UCL), certainly fit this description. The lab's XenoCells project (pp 90–95) oscillates between prototypical column, colourful coral and impasto aggregate. The clear outline of the column is articulated in multiple corrugated ruffles, rucks and pleats of varying translucencies and luminous colourations. In 'Affects of Intricate Mass' (pp 72–6), Roland Snooks unveils the RMIT Mace – an example of an object that possesses a familiar primitive morphology (the club, or mace, being one of the most archaic of weapons) while simultaneously being corrupted, compromised and corroded in its silhouette by a rich, massively intricate maze of beautifully swirling plications of fibrous components. Both XenoCells and the RMIT Mace celebrate the 'excessive resolution' that Carpo speaks of.

A Hidden Tool

One of the major differences between the process-oriented production of architectural pieces around the turn of the 21st century and the desires, ambitions and interests of the next generation of architects is certainly the dismissal of the tool as a means to shape the architectural discourse. A debate that inspects the manifold facets of the post-digital age such as ideas about architecture as an autonomous object, interest in phenomenological qualities, the disentanglement of contextualisation and object, and speculative and weird realism.

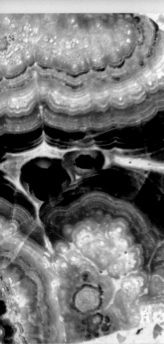

Mies van der Rohe,
Detail of onyx wall,
Villa Tugendhat,
Brno,
Czech Republic,
1930

Mies van der Rohe trained
as a stonemason in his
father's workshop in Aachen,
Germany. In stark contrast to
his reduced formal repertoire
of planes and volumes, the
stone in his work emanates
drama, swirling motion and
profound chatter. There is a
quasi-romantic side to Mies
after all.

For example, in The Bittertang Farm's Buru Buru project (see the article by Bittertang cofounder Michael Loverich on pp 102–7), the re-emerging interest in the primitive hut is interpreted in steel and straw. The almost repulsive quality of the intrusively bulging, ugly brownish straw 'sausages' somehow ties in with what Schopenhauer described in the early 19th century as the stimulating and the charming. Although Schopenhauer considers the stimulating a contemplation-resistant object,[7] Buru Buru can certainly be described as charming, in its pastoral moments virtuously contemplating the repertoire of memory, the picturesque, and romantic desires. It also effortlessly escapes discussions on technique, and rather lives through its physical presence, engaging not only with its visual context, but also with its tactile and probably olfactory qualities.

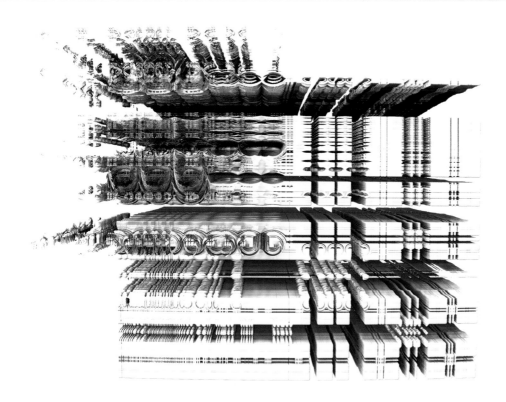

SPAN (Matias del Campo
and Sandra Manninger),
Blocks – Topview,
Detroit,
2016

top: Blocks speculates on the nature of urban textures.
The project negotiates in a bland space a combination
of the conceptual and the actual. The strikingly familiar
features interrogate primordial architectural problems and
parse them as strange corners, ruthless blocks, coquette
windows, firm symmetries, fluffy colonnades, sublime
naves and all the intimate relationships between them,
regardless of their scale.

Canaletto, *Venice: Caprice View of Piazzetta
with the Horses of San Marco,*
c 1743

bottom: Capriccio painting is primarily defined by the invention
of architectural scapes that organise real elements into unfamiliar
and speculative alternatives. Canaletto's capriccio creates a
convincing alternative universe in which the horses occupy the
Piazzetta. It is a familiar yet alien sight that evokes an uneasy
tension between horses, plinths, steps, dogs and the soignée
Venetians who seem to contemplate the strange appearance
of four horses without riders. The Baroque exercise of the
architectural capriccio can be considered an early form of
negotiating realism through the lens of speculation.

Adolf Loos,
American Bar,
Vienna,
1908

Material agencies are defined
as the main generators
of mood in architectural
discourse. Adolf Loos is
an exemplary icon for
this argument, able to
orchestrate sensations by
using the inherent spectacular
characteristics of material
properties such as stone
striations, reflectivity and the
tactility of bronze and leather.

However, atmosphere is created by more than just visual perception. MONAD Studio considers the perception of sound to be crucial in all its diverse incarnations. The design research practice's various exercises in the transmutation of sound into architecture are manifested in the multitude of exotically formed interpretations of various string and pipe instruments. Cofounder Eric Goldemberg's essay 'Mood, Posture and Rhythmic Feedback, (pp 108–17) is not only an account of how these sonic beasts came into existence; it also reflects on the relationship between sound and body, exemplified in the discovery of feedback as a musical technique by the immortal Jimmy Hendrix.

In a conversation about the nature of feedback between object and subject in some of Coop Himmelb(l)au's early work (pp 46–53), cofounder Wolf D Prix provides an insight into the driving forces behind some of the group's radical installations, such as Hard Space (1970) – albeit he still, and rightfully so, prefers to look forward instead of back. It seems there is a multitude of explanatory models for the different aspects of 'mood' in architectural production, and indeed Marjan Colletti delivers in his essay 'The Awesome and Capricious Language of Past, Present and Future Digital Moods' (pp 118–25) a highly detailed forensic analysis of the term. Etymological considerations and the lingual specifics of the expression serve as a launching pad for a plethora of thoughts on its ontology and use in symbolic culture at large.

Andrew Saunders, on the other hand, interrogates the historical dimension of 'mood' (*Stimmung*) and 'will to art' (*Kunstwollen*). His article, 'Figuring Mood: The Role of *Stimmung* in the Formal Approach of Heinrich Wölfflin and Alois Riegl' (pp 34–41) illuminates the relationship between the thinking models of Wölfflin, the doyen of Baroque art theory, and Alois Riegl, the main proponent of Formalism in fin-de-siècle Vienna. Saunders thus treads a line between late 19th-century and current modes of design thinking. Both Saunders and Colletti circumscribe the navigational charts on which the speculative projects in this Δ find their ground, a very useful cartographic achievement that helps readers navigate safely through the sometimes murky yet adventurous waters that this issue has to offer.

In a Mood for Architecture

Evoking through design tends to be underdiscussed in conventional architectural discourse. There is always the chance to slip into the esoteric, putting such an idea forward that to a certain extent can be considered absolutely subjective. But that would be an outdated mode of thinking, as it would position human beings at the centre of every perception. Novel conversations on subject-to-object and object-to-object relationships are required that yield the opportunity to observe the problem through a speculative lens. In this universe of thinking, a set of architectural properties can evoke mood. On the other hand, do objects in themselves have a mood? This issue of Δ poses these and other related questions through a group of architects whose work, either intentionally or coincidentally, tackles the problem from the vantage point of speculative realism. Δ

Notes
1. Ian Bogost, *Alien Phenomenology, Or What It's Like to Be a Thing*, University of Minnesota Press (Minneapolis, MN and London), 2012, Kindle Edition, Location 701 of 4016.
2. Thomas Mann, *Der Zauberberg* (*The Magic Mountain*), S Fischer Verlag (Frankfurt), 1924, p 877.
3. Mario Carpo, *The Digital Turn in Architecture 1992–2012*, John Wiley & Sons Chichester), 2012.
4. Sylvia Lavin, 'In a Contemporary Mood', in Zaha Hadid and Patrik Schumacher (eds), *Latent Utopias: Experiments Within Contemporary Architecture*, Steirischer Herbst (Graz), 2002, p 49.
5. Todd Gannon and N Katherine Hayles, 'Mood Swings: The Aesthetics of Ambient Emergence', in Neil Brooks and Josh Toth (eds), *The Mourning After: Attending the Wake of Postmodernism*, Ropodi (Amsterdam), 2007, p 133.
6. Graham Harman, *Weird Realism: Lovecraft and Philosophy*, Zero Books Winchester and Washington DC), 2012.
7. Arthur Schopenhauer, *The World as Will and Representation*, Dover Publications, Mineola, NY), 1966, p 187.

Mood Swings

Architectural Affective Disorder

What is architectural mood? Is it subjective, or objective? Phenomenological, or conceptual? Consistent, or constantly evolving? **John McMorrough**, Associate Professor of Architecture at the University of Michigan, here considers the theme from four different angles – indicative, imperative, interrogative and subjunctive. He suggests that we are embarking on a 'manic' phase, in which the noise of modern life makes making an impression ever more difficult, but the vocabulary of mood in architecture just might be growing richer as a result.

John McMorrough

The unprecedented expansion of the concept of freedom of thought … has led to any number of unpleasant developments, but none more disconcerting than the fact that place, once that most fixed of entities, has now become a matter of personal opinion.

— Fran Lebowitz, *Social Studies*, 1977[1]

far left
Claude Monet,
*Rouen Cathedral,
West Façade,*
1894

left
Claude Monet,
*Rouen Cathedral,
West Façade,
Sunlight,*
1894

right
Claude Monet,
*The Portal of
Rouen Cathedral
in Morning Light,*
1894

In the 1890s, Monet painted Rouen Cathedral in a series of canvases to capture the atmospheric variations of different times, dates and weather conditions, and their influence on perceptions of the edifice, such that the relation of subject and object in their affective dimension became inseparable.

After literally thousands of years of development, architecture has resolved some things. The descriptions of its means, its geometry, its codes and procedures (though subject to changes in tools and technology) are relatively established; it is a discipline of specification and control. Also, the question of architectural ends, though continuing to occupy some attention, has stabilised over time, as throughout its various manifestations (personal or collective, utopian or managerial) architecture fundamentally operates as the provision of shelter and division. The correlation of these means and ends is less clear. For a discourse of description (which architecture is, both conceptually and historically), the attempts to find a definitive resolution of this relationship (an ongoing rumination) are generators of much debate and development.

Unlike a painting or a poem, where to comprehend the work in an idiosyncratic manner is encouraged, in architecture the aspiration (admitted or not) is for the work to be experientially coherent (even as an expression of multiplicity). An oft-cited claim is that various art forms (including architecture) aspire to the condition of music. Underlying this claim is the attribution to the medium of music of an affective purity, such that the layperson can be aesthetically moved, without the necessity of any knowledge of the disciplinary logic by which the affect is formed. As the philosopher Gottfried Leibniz relates: 'music is the pleasure the human mind experiences from counting without being aware that it is counting.'[2] In architecture, the claim to such parity with music speaks to an ambition that privileges emotion and sensation, but also manipulation. Embedded within this aspiration of architecture to the condition of music is, also, a desire for a totalisation of response. This is where 'mood' enters into architecture's deliberation of affect as both solution and question.

Herman van Swanevelt,
Building with a Square Tower,
c 1630s

Over the course of the 1630s, the Dutch artist Van Swanevelt made a series of etchings of the 'Italianate landscape' that contributed to the popularisation of such images in Northern Europe.

Indicative Mood (Indicating a State of Reality)

On initial consideration, mood seems like a rather trivial concern upon which to base serious architectural discourse. Mood sits lightly in the range of human reactions; it has been described as little more than feelings. It is something that is understood as a personal reaction. But mood also exists as a condition of language (as in the mood of a piece of writing, or the technical description of the mood of verb tenses, which indicate a state of being or reality). Seen from the perspective of modern psychiatry, mood acts as a conditioning of how we understand the world around us.[3] Mood, then, is not only a personal reaction to a particular space (a phenomenological concern), but also a medium of affective content (a conceptual issue). In its consideration, a whole set of rather fundamental questions arise: the relationship of subject and object, the source of causation, and the universality of reaction. A serious consideration of mood moves quite quickly from something understood as trifling and subject to change (one speaks of a 'shifting mood') to a deliberation regarding influence and affect. In short, mood, once evoked, provokes.

As a topic so seemingly central to the idea of architecture it seems that mood would be found throughout architecture's history. In periods of change (technological, ideological, stylistic), not to mention the changes in the cultural milieu in which it operates (too numerous to mention), it can be argued that architecture's particular moods have changed specifically in relation to a fluctuating economy of attention. The temple, the ruin, the cathedral are but a few among countless other versions of architecture that have dealt with mood by implication. At the beginning of the 20th century, German socialist Georg Simmel identified the 'blasé attitude' of the newly constituted metropolitan subject, who, in response to being confronted with ever-increasing stimuli from the environment, ignores it.[4] This diagnosis, one of many, identified the ever-increasing amount of agitation required in the realm of cultural production to rise above the din and create an impression upon the subject. Since then there have been a variety of affective gambits enacted in relation to cultural context, explicitly as either intensification or amelioration.

To consider mood as a proper subject in the contemporary moment, one needs to frame the issue against more recent developments.

Herman van Swanevelt,
Ruined Building with a Tower,
c 1630s

As one of the first to artistically depict such landscapes without allegorical or mythological subjects, Van Swanevelt's series of buildings in landscape represents a study of mood as setting.

Imperative Mood (Indicating a State of Command)

To consider mood as a proper subject in the contemporary moment, one needs to frame the issue against more recent developments. Historically, it was 'style' that described the effect of a building, and the coherence of its elements. Stylistic categorisation was the frame looking towards the object, its appearance and our perception of it. Since the waning of an integrated relation between style and period, the development of the architectural avant-garde has been motivated by the question of an adequate historical correlation between moment and formal manifestation.[5] The late 20th-century 'postmodern' approach to architecture as a language was one attempt to gain a conventionalised relation between form and connotation. The limit of this approach, in its reliance on the existence of a received vocabulary, is that it constricts both innovation and speciation of architectural effects as the recombination of givens. It is in response to the relativity of linguistically based models of apprehending architecture that mood (or rather the concept of mood) is seen to bring a different sort of exchange, one that offers less than communication, but more than feeling. In the long turn away from codification (the language of architectural formula) and towards more idiomatic expressions (the parole of specific works), mood comes in as a replacement for interpretive meaning systems, for expressions that are more direct and give us a means of understanding, without the necessity of decoding. In discussing mood, the architectural theorist Jeffrey Kipnis has been known to comment (on various occasions) that architecture has a long history of invoking the mood of reverence, but much less so any others.[6] As if to fill the gaps of architecture's affective capacities, considerable recent attention has been focused on the elaboration of a more extensive range of possibility. With an awareness of mood we see its proliferation, and in giving specific attention to the subject, mood has elicited a widening of affective manifestations within architecture, into increasingly nuanced expression, in its sublimity but also into diverse and unexpected dispositions (aggressive, cheerful, rapturous, perky, repulsive). Inspired in equal parts by philosophical developments and creative opportunity, the discourse of moody architecture that has emerged has focused on colouration, nonstandard repetitions and 'artifactuality'.[7]

Herman van Swanevelt,
View of a Ruined Building,
c 1630s

Characteristic of Van Swanevelt's pictures was the interrelationship among three parts: settings, buildings and people, all with variations of lighting depicting different times of day.

Interrogative Mood (Indicating a State of Questioning)

In parsing the effect of mood in architecture, the framework may be less relevant to the particularity of one mood than to the intensity and duration of its fluctuations. From the perspective of the collective and discursive (that is, the discipline) it is clear there is not a mood, but many, which are not stable entities, but change quickly from one to another. From a medical perspective such rapid changes in emotional state, colloquially known as 'mood swings', are, in the technical diagnosis of their most intense forms, categorised as manic depression, which is one of a set of affective disorders, including anxiety disorder, depression and bipolar disorder (another term for manic depression). Those so affected are subject to fits of exuberance, but might also be placid for long periods. One may be either wildly productive or listless.[8] For a fitful discipline like architecture, perhaps affective disorder is a useful interpretive lens through which to view the slow inflection of similar temperament over the course of the 20th century into increasingly rapid changes in the contemporary moment.[9]

Over time, mood has been attributed to the brain, to the heart, to the humours, to the environment and to chemistry.[10] In this accounting it is possible to identify foreshadowing of the current idea of mood in architecture (as significant emanation with an ambiguous origination) within these earlier conceptualisations. Paralleling the trajectory of architecture understood not only in relation to changes in society, economics and technology, there are not only many moods, but also many ideas of what mood is and how it is described. The relation of emotion, mood and affect is not a given.[11] The sporadic development of mood's description has fostered the introduction of new vocabularies, and in so doing the concept of mood and its causation has transformed.[12]

Subjunctive Mood (Indicating a Hypothetical State)

The idea of mood in architecture, once identified, transforms in its significance and changes in its origination, and the mood of architecture as discussed thus far cannot be considered merely as a function of the object, but also of its (discursive) context. This would understand mood not as the expression of an authorial intention, nor directly of cultural forces, but as the affective field of the architectural discipline itself, a disembodied collective of various bodies (schools, journals and so on). This is a line of thinking in which, at one moment, one understands the object, that is, the building, as inert matter, and at still another moment as a personification of cultural attributes and economic forces, and finally, as a being unto itself. The reductio ad absurdum of the argument of mood is not that certain architectures invoke certain moods, or that architecture as a field reacts to its cultural environment to make and describe architecture of a certain temperament, or even to have an exacerbation of moody effects as a source of creative inspiration; the implication in extremis of mood in architecture is that the buildings themselves, those collections of inert materials, have moods, of which the inhabitants are only partial recipients.[13]

The attentive elaboration of mood, its affects and its vocabulary, could have a therapeutic effect for architecture, even if it is subject to change.

ood is either 'in here' or 'out there', the absolutely internal gic of the discipline of architecture, or a complete projection to it (a fiction of personification). Regardless, the awareness mood both expands and deepens architectural possibility. xpands as it increases the ways in which we can imagine uildings acting, and deepens in that, in contrast to the ckground noise condition that is endemic to architecture, e can imagine instead the generation of wildly varying mospheres. Read as such, we see increasing shifts of mperament in the long emergence of the discipline of chitecture. The fluctuations of mood, its diverse relations d causations, originations and affects should be understood manifestations of a volatile volition. In these increasingly pid shifts, the attentive elaboration of mood, its affects and vocabulary, could have a therapeutic effect for architecture, en if it is subject to change. ∆

far left
*Statue of a Kore
(The Elgin Kore),
c 475 BC*

left
*Fragmentary Head of
Epikouros Worked for
Insertion in a Bust,
c AD 100-150*

below
*Torso of Actaeon,
c 1st-2nd century*

The phases of Greek sculpture, from the Archaic (with a focus on the kouroi, or standing male nude – the female counterpart of which was the kore (with a more naturalised pose), to the Classical (with its more realistic depictions of subjects), to the Hellenistic (with its more realistic depictions of subjects), represent the development of technique and affect. In their fragmentary status, sculptures such as these rehearse, before the fact, contemporary dilemmas of mood as questions of material, figuration and perception.

Notes
1. Fran Lebowitz, *Social Studies*, Pocket Books (New York), 1977, p 87.
2. As quoted in Oliver Sacks, *The Man who Mistook his Wife for a Hat*, Summit Books (New York), 1985, p 205.
3. Karina Grudnikov, 'How Your Mood Influences Your Corporeal Sensations', *Psychology Today*, 44, July 2011, p 42.
4. Georg Simmel, 'The Metropolis and Mental Life' [1903] in *Georg Simmel on Individuality and Social Form*, University of Chicago Press (Chicago, IL), 1972, pp 324–39.
5. Manfredo Tafuri, 'Architecture as "Indifferent Object" and the Crisis of Critical Attention', in *Theories and History of Architecture*, Granada (London), 1980, pp 79–102.
6. Such an aphorismic pronouncement escapes categorical verification, yet one has the feeling that it is true. In the extensive bibliography of Jeffrey Kipnis's contribution to the discussion of contemporary architectural mood, perhaps the most complete elaboration, and emphatic response to his own question about the affective range of architecture can be found in the essay for the catalogue of the 2002 exhibition 'Mood River', for which he was author, editor and curator. See Jeffrey Kipnis, 'On Those Who Step Into The Same River …', *Mood River*, Wexner Center for the Arts (Columbus, OH), 2002, pp 34–44.
7. See Matias del Campo and Sandra Manninger, 'Artifact and Affect: Open-Ended Strata of Communication', in Tuba Kocatürk and Benachir Medjdoub (eds), *Distributed Intelligence in Design*, Wiley-Blackwell Publishing (Chichester), 2011, pp 99–105.
8. Healthline, 'Affective Disorders (Mood Disorders)': www.healthline.com/health/affective-disorders.
9. Architectural theorist Sylvia Lavin has previously published an essay with a title quite similar to the present effort. See Sylvia Lavin, 'The New Mood of Affective Disorder', *Assemblage*, 41, April 2000, p 40. While the author is an avid follower of Lavin, especially in regard to the topic of architecture and mood, it should also be noted that the argument and scope of the two texts are quite different (with all debt, of influence and coincidence fully acknowledged).
10. Kenneth Davison, 'Historical Aspects of Mood Disorders', *Psychiatry*, 5 (4), April 2006, pp 115–18.
11. Laura Sizer, 'Towards a Computational Theory of Mood', *The British Journal for the Philosophy of Science*, 51 (4), December 2000, pp 734–69.
12. See Åsa Jansson, 'Mood Disorders and the Brain: Depression, Melancholia, and the Historiography of Psychiatry', *Medical History*, 55, 2011, pp 393–9.
13. For a starting point in surveying the burgeoning philosophical literature on 'object oriented ontology', see Graham Harman, *The Quadruple Object*, Zero Books (Alresford), 2011.

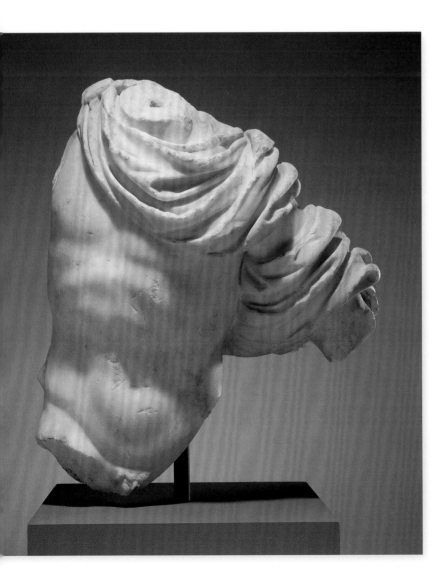

Eragatory,
case study interior II,
2016

Interior space study exploring
the juxtaposition of the same
texture contrasting through
different geometries, materials
and continuity.

Isaie Bloch

!ntimacy

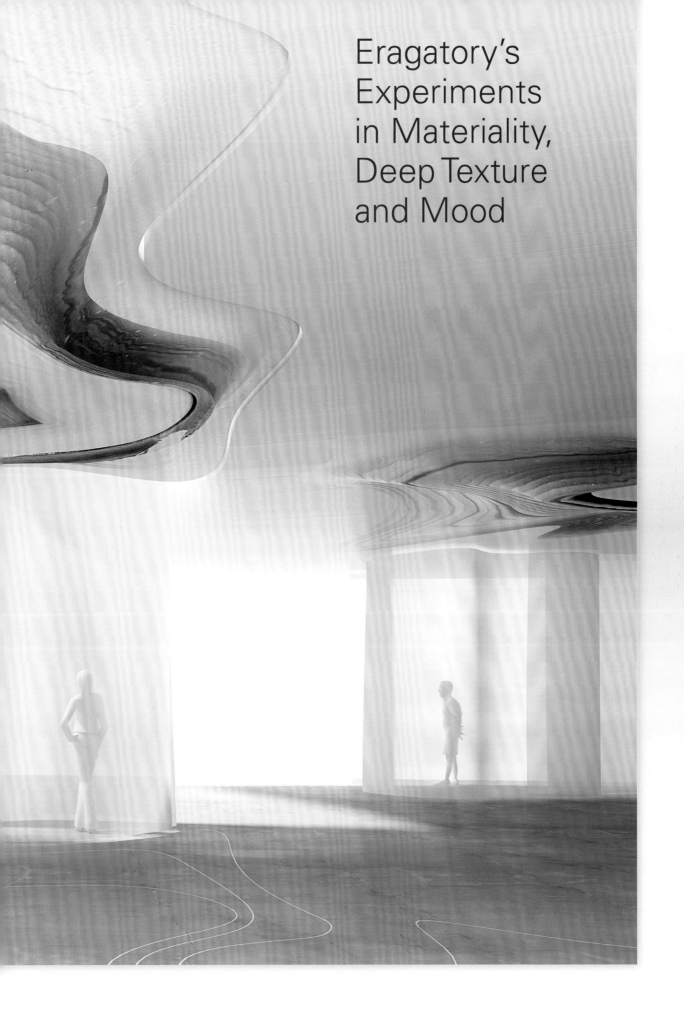

Eragatory's Experiments in Materiality, Deep Texture and Mood

Because of their textural and sensory qualities – even or uneven, smooth or rough, cold or warm, reflective or matt – particular materials tend to evoke particular moods. But this does not mean that their nature and structure cannot be played with in order to create surprising atmospheres. London-based design practice Eragatory's '!ntimacy' series of interiors does just that, producing visual anomalies that distort the viewer's material understanding of space. **Isaie Bloch**, the firm's founder, describes how.

The notion of deep texture that characterises the London-based design practice Eragatory's '!ntimacy' series plays with the idea that texture, materiality and geometry do not intrinsically relate to each other, while they heavily inform our perception of an object. The series stresses the discontinuity of our rather inert physical perception against its more sensitive ambient reading. Craftsmen would argue that material properties dictate form to a large extent, while we conceptualise and design an object or a space in a digital non-material environment. This static understanding of the sensorial relationships between an object and its material relies solely on our cognitive understanding of that particular object.

Eragatory,
private commission
for a one-bedroom
flat refurbishment,
London,
2016

The saturated floor pattern locally shifts into a geometrical anomaly, transitioning from floor to a subtle extruded border condition and eventually wall; this while keeping a continuous texture. The bathtub on the other hand extrudes the texture in a vertical planar way and by doing so only reflects a local colour instead of a texture.

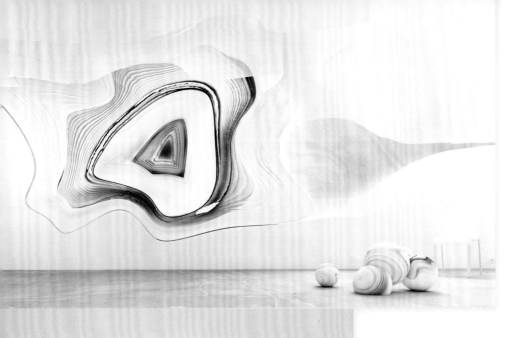

Eragatory,
case study interior
III, 2016

Nested wall feature producing
the illusion of depth and relief
through the coloured texture
in the middle, while it is only
the outer geometry that has
actual relief using an offset of
the inner texture.

Material Maquillage

Textural qualities which are catalysts for our perception of architectural ambience have mostly been related to the actual material an object is made of. Marble produces heterogeneity, the colour of wood can either refer to a warm floaty atmosphere or a dark oppressing space, stone columns give us a sense of solidity, glass and steel combined evoke a vast and endless sensation. When new, optimised or cheaper building materials arise we often tend to change their material appearance by cladding them in a series of false textures, so as to make them visually relate to other existing materials which consequently impact our perception. As an example: a faux-marble, plaster-covered concrete column tries to evoke the feeling of a solid sturdy marble column, which is what we would recognise to make structural, ornamental and spatial sense. But as it is merely a texture, it could have been applied to any other structural object which geometrically would not align with something produced out of marble. Due to this we could very easily cover a steel space frame in faux marble; yet we don't, as this totally decontextualises the object. The lightweight space frame would suddenly feel fragile because of its textural qualities, while keeping its material strength. Our understanding of space could be dramatically distorted if we were to play out these textural differences more.

Eragatory,
case study interior I, 2016

Passage showing a juxtaposition between
the actual initial raw object in the back, in
its natural non-modified form; the same
Carrara texture generating geometry while
being fabricated in a non-textural material on
the right wall; and a designed pinched edge
condition using only the 2D impression of that
same marble texture.

Textural Discontinuity

Another indulgent aspect texture can create is the illusion of a higher resolution, without making the actual object geometrically complex. This geometrical complexity – which is often associated to a certain extent with excess, saturation or chaos – is mostly applied in a very singular and linear way. Designers and architects either produce geometrical complexity with very plain textural qualities so as to read the geometry, or they texturise rather simple geometries so as to enhance their visual complexity. But they never really transition between the two or disrupt both concepts.

The interior speculations of '!ntimacy' play with the idea that architectural objects could initially be non-material and non-textural in order to allow geometries to have a subverted relationship to their material and textural qualities. This borrows from the approach operated by scenic designers, CG artists and the plastic arts, in which most artefacts are designed through an acontextual and rather abstract representation of a mood, rather than in a material purist framework. The case studies use a set of subverted rules to define an object and space in its relationship with texture.

The case studies use a set of subverted rules to define an object and space in its relationship with texture.

below
Eragatory,
case study interior VII
2016

Drop-down ceiling, producing resolution simultaneously through the geometrical articulation of certain areas in relationship to the saturation of texture and resolution through texture only. Both types of articulation and the local deformations distort our material understanding of the space.

Eragatory,
case study interior VI,
2016

Example of a dome-like space
where all the sensorial material
properties of the objects defining
the space lose their material
behaviour. Both the object in
the space and the architectural
elements echo the same unusual
textural impressions and textural
resolution without reflecting
any material properties.

Distorting Effect and Reality

Throughout designing the !ntimacy series,
contradictions in relationship to the hierarchy
of texture as being a mere effect rather than a
geometrical reality have triggered an ambiguous
relationship, where all are equally significant
rather than being detached layers of information.

Form can prevail independent of material or
textural properties. Texture dramatically affects
our sensorial understanding of a primitive or
complex form, conversely to a complex geometry
without texture which tries to be read by itself.
Deep or geometrical texture can produce spatial
articulation independent of its actual texture or
initial material.

Deep texture, oversaturation and non-material
behaviours ultimately result in a sophisticated
architectural production, distorting our
understanding of mood. They generate a platform-
biasing effect or reality, ambience or sensorial
qualities, projection or displacement. ⌂

The Khaleesi Tower
─────────────────────

WEST 57TH STREET, NYC

Aesthetics
as
Politics

Mark Foster Gage Architects,
Tower on West 57th Street
('The Khaleesi'),
New York City,
2015

The project is not only differentiated
from the local context by height, but
also by high-resolution detail that
invites curiosity rather than providing
for an immediately understandable
architectural one-liner.

Has the discipline of architecture gone too far down the route of practicality and pragmatism? New York-based architect **Mark Foster Gage** argues that the focus on aspects such as programme, context and sustainability has become so great as to leave little space for truly inspirational creativity. And yet current technology is opening up possibilities for unprecedentedly bold and awe-inspiring additions to the built environment. Love it or loathe it, could visionary proposals like his firm's Khaleesi Tower – with its mixture of high-resolution detail and ethereal transparency – be the way forward?

On 8 June 1972, Associated Press photographer Nick Ut captured the iconic image of a nine-year-old girl, Phan Thi Kim Phuc, who, naked and screaming, was photographed running towards the camera having been severely burnt by a South Vietnamese napalm attack. On 5 June 1989, photographer Jeff Widener captured 'the unknown rebel', a Chinese dissident, standing defiantly in front of a line of tanks in Tiananmen Square, Beijing. On 29 May 1913, Russian composer Igor Stravinsky debuted his recent composition *The Rite of Spring* before a packed theatre in Paris. So radical was the dissonant and unfamiliar performance that theatregoers soon began to hurl vegetables and other objects towards the stage, leading to a violent street riot.

It does not happen very often, but occasionally, in just the right circumstances, an image or creative act can, against the stacked odds of cynicism and apathy, change the world. In these particular cases an image could galvanise an anti-Vietnam war movement in the US, or illustrate to the citizens of China that another form of life was possible – one of peaceful resistance. Or a musical composition, lasting less than two hours, could prompt a riot that would open the minds of an entire generation to the possibility of entirely new forms of music.

The high-resolution detail of the base disappears into silhouette profile as the project rises.

opposite: Greater levels of detail appear on areas where humans are positioned to see them up close.

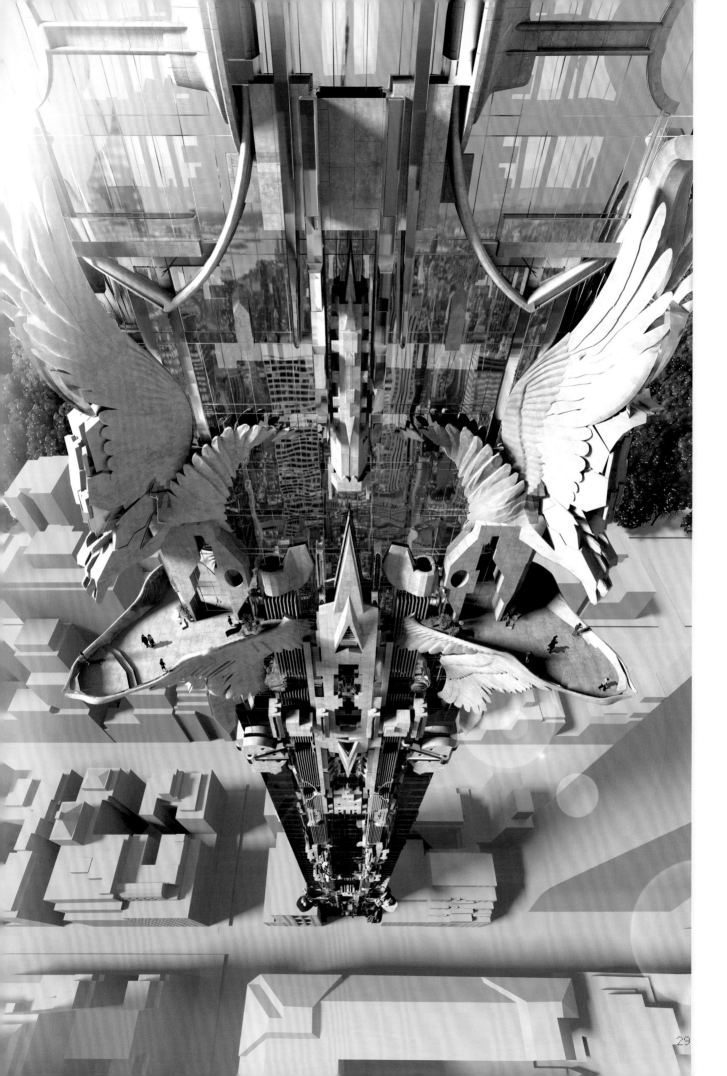

Milky opaque glass at the bottom of the structure produces a monolithic reading at the base, which becomes more transparent and ethereal as the project rises.

The massive mid-rise balconies are accessed from a limited suite of retail and culinary amenities within the sky lobby.

While forgotten by many, architecture is, in fact, a creative act. And yet the power of architecture and its imagery to prompt change exists only as architectural myth and ancient lore – a power associated only with the Miesian gods of yesteryear, a magic no longer known or practised. Instead, architects today focus on simpler problems, more local problems, problems of context (it looks like the mountains in the distance), of programme (put a Starbucks in the bathroom), of marketing-friendly animal metaphors (it's a bird), or how to consume a bit less energy (mom look – LEED copper). Like a decrepit sorceress robbed of her powers, architecture sits mute in a world of technologically enabled explosive possibilities, vaguely remembering having had, in the past, perhaps more respect, more prestige and certainly a lot more power.

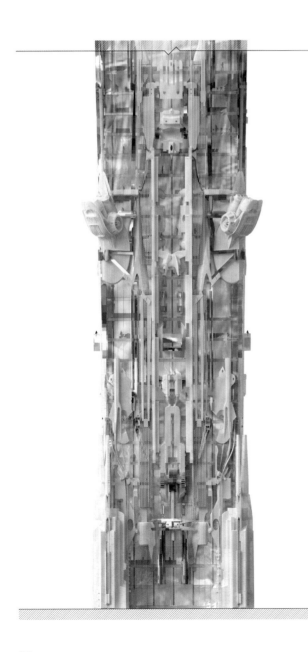

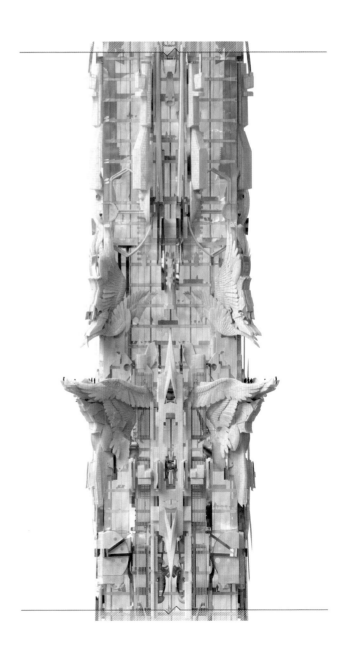

The mid-rise exterior balconies align with the top of the Empire State Building.

The power of architecture and its imagery to prompt change exists only as architectural myth and ancient lore

Residents enter the project at ground level while retail customers access the shopping area from adjacent exterior grand stairs. Artwork in collaboration with Patrick Faulwetter.

Mark Foster Gage Architects believes that change is coming, that architects are slowly tiring of the clever diagrams, metaphors of buildings looking like animals, or the insistence that architecture is merely easy, or just fun, or 'yes', or whatever the sound bite *du jour* is. Any attempt to distil architecture into a smaller, bite-sized anything denies the reality of its reach, complexity and potential depth and vastness. Instead of becoming smaller, easier or infantilisingly 'funner', architecture is poised to re-enter culture with a technologically enabled ferocity not seen since the Renaissance. Our office may not be the cause, or even a player, but we will have a voice – one that is louder than diagrams, more confrontational than birds, more inspiring than LEED copper and, above all, serious about the emerging potentials of architecture to once again inspire shifts along the fundamental fault lines of culture. The sorceress awakens. And she's pissed.

In this spirit we invite you to view these images of our Tower on West 57th Street project. You may not understand it or what we are trying to do, for it does not aim to solve any clever problems of context, offers no exhibitionist intertwinings of programme, has no cute animalistic metaphors, and is of course LEED Titanium, but not *about* being LEED Titanium. We anticipate that if successful, you will either love or hate these images with a vehemence usually reserved for politics or conversations about abortion. We welcome your love or hatred, and suspect that if you have gotten this far, we have already won, as we have not been ignored. ᗡ

top: An interior grand stair connects the residential entrance level with the retail areas on floors two to four. Artwork in collaboration with Patrick Faulwetter.

left: The mid-rise sky lobby has a restaurant that is accessed through symmetrical escalators that ascend from below into the dining and balcony-access areas above. Artwork in collaboration with Patrick Faulwetter.

Andrew Saunders

Figuring Mood

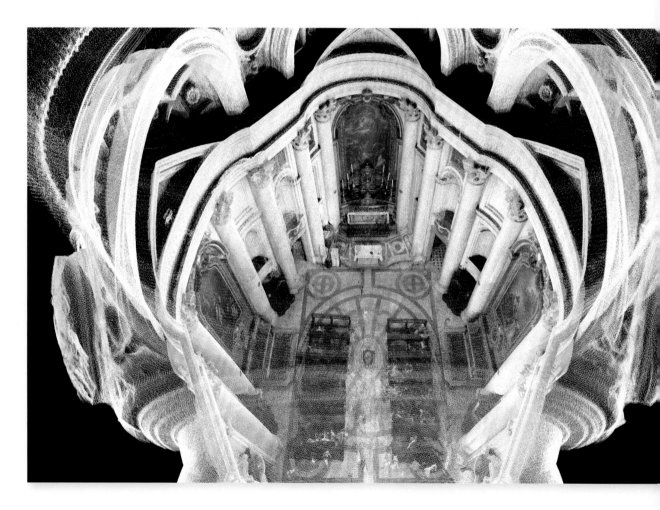

The Role of *Stimmung* in the Formal Approach of Heinrich Wölfflin and Alois Riegl

ary Polk, John Darby, Chao
iu, Natasha Sanjaya, Esther
a, Ping Wang, Sum Cheng,
rdeep Gujral, Doug Breuer,
hui Gan, Kunil Paik, Elsa
istiani and Shen Shicheng,
efracted Objects (Studio
ndrew Saunders, PennDesign,
niversity of Pennsylvania),
015

collection of physical models is
inted from ruled-surface figures
computational light refraction
mulations.

Roughly translatable as 'mood' or 'atmosphere', *Stimmung* plays a key part in the late-19th-century writings of German art historians Wölfflin and Riegl. **Andrew Saunders**, Associate Professor of Architecture at the University of Pennsylvania School of Design, studies the origins of the concept, which links rational perceptions of harmony with notions of emotional response. He examines the two writers' contrasting views of *Stimmung* in relation to the Baroque, and highlights its little-acknowledged role in the inception of formalism.

ancesco Borromini,
urch of San Carlo alle Quattro
ntane, Rome,
nsecrated 1646

posite: This view from a 3D laser-scanned digital
odel of the interior of this Baroque church perfectly
ustrates Wölfflin's description of the mood of
roque interior space: 'In a baroque building man
swallowed up by the colossal space that engulfs
m: it is on this principle that the baroque interior is
signed.' (*Renaissance and Baroque* [*Renaissance
d Baroque*, 1888], trans Kathrin Simon, Collins
ondon), 1964, p 62)

Ideas can only be explicitly stated, but moods [*Stimmungen*] can also be conveyed with architectural forms; at any rate, every style imparts a more or less definite mood [*Stimmung*].
– Heinrich Wölfflin, 1888[1]

The ultimate appeal of assessing architecture through mood is the powerful promise of reception through synaesthesia: the production of a sense impression relating to one sense or part of the body by stimulation of another sense or part of the body, including the mind. Due to its inevitable physicality, architecture is dependent on the sensorial relay between the physical and the ephemeral for evoking mood. As an epistemological mode of perception, mood operates between both the objective and subjective, or rather emotional and intellectual perception. The etymology of the English word 'mood' stems from the Old English *mod* alluding to both mind and the outward expression of emotion.[2] The German word for mood, *Stimmung*, for which there is no equivalent translation in English, has a far more holistic definition originating in Pythagoras's (570–495 BC) musical concept of a world harmony. Philologist Leo Spitzer (1887–1990) dedicated an entire volume to tracing its origin and meaning as 'the unity of feelings experienced by man face to face with his environment (a landscape, nature, one's fellow man), and would comprehend and weld together the objective (factual) and the subjective (psychological) into one harmonious unity'. For Spitzer, the modern 'death' of the full concept of the word was due to 'the growth of analytical rationalism and the segmentary, fragmentary, materialistic, and positivistic view of the world'.[3] Due to this fragmentation, the contemporary definition of mood has many different associations within different disciplines including psychology, physiology, philosophy, aesthetics and design. What links the concept across disciplines is its role in the perception of objects.

To better understand the capacity of mood in architecture, we must first examine how the burgeoning field of psychology of perception played a critical role in the pioneering work of art historians Heinrich Wölfflin (1864–1945) and Alois Riegl (1858–1905). Both used mood as a critical instrument for combating relativism and reassessing the agency of certain periods of art and architecture, including the Baroque, which previously resisted analysis through established classical canons of beauty. Due to their emphasis on formal elements to link the visual aspect of perceptual psychology, their experimental approach marked the beginning of formalism in art and architecture. The formal project of Wölfflin and Riegl has a rich and long trajectory in architecture including such figures as Sigfried Giedion, Erwin Panofsky, Rudolf Wittkower, Colin Rowe and Peter Eisenman, to name only a few, but the pivotal role of mood in the birth of formalism is rarely highlighted. Furthermore, when brought to the forefront, we can re-evaluate mood as an important unifying concept in contemporary design outside of analytical rationalism and overly determined perception of objects.

Pythagorean Origins of *Stimmung*: Part-to-Whole in Architecture

The meaning of *Stimmung* is derived from the German verb *stimmen* and is associated with tuning and voice. It evolved from an early Pythagorean concept of world harmony. For the Pythagoreans, there existed a musical harmony in planets and stars reflecting a godly movement in nature and human art. Their 'theological' approach, patterned on music, interwove science and mythology and would prove highly translatable to architecture due to the transposition between mystical concepts and rational numbers. Since reducible to numbers, music, arithmetic, astronomy and geometry were all linked.

In architecture, the Pythagorean numerical translation of world harmony would prove influential in the canonical writing of Vitruvius (*c* 80–*c* 15 BC). His treatise on efficient technical production, formal composition and innovation is all rooted in the ontological priority of cosmic harmony.[4] When Vitruvius writes 'Order gives due measure to the members of work considered separately, and symmetrical agreement to the proportions of the whole',[5] the emphasis on harmonious part-to-whole composition is an allegiance to the Pythagorean principle.

The Pythagorean numerical translation of world harmony would be revived and adapted to humanistic concerns in the Renaissance, particularly in the writings of Leon Battista Alberti (1404–1472). Echoing Vitruvius, Alberti writes: 'I shall define Beauty to be a Harmony of all the Parts, in whatsoever Subject it appears, fitted together with such Proportion and Connection, that nothing could be added, diminished or altered, but for the Worse.'[6] The classical and Renaissance definition of the harmonic ratio of part to whole would become the canon by which beauty was to be measured until the late 19th century.

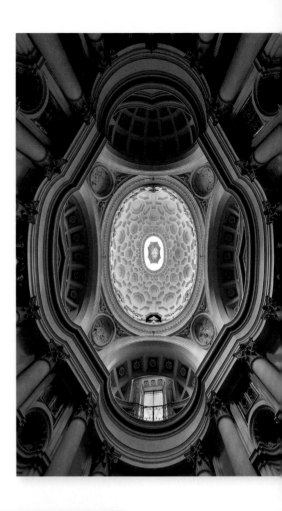

Francesco Borromini, Church of San Carlo alle Quattro Fontane, Rome, consecrated 1646

above: Wölfflin describes the mood of Baroque geometry: 'The oval is restless and seems always on the point of change.' (*Renaissance and Baroque, op cit,* p 113)

Giovanni Paolo Panini, *Interior of St Peter's, Rome,* 1757

left: For Wölfflin, the painterly effect is dependent on the theatrical manipulation of light and shadow, chiaroscuro: 'It is the Baroque that first uses light as an essential element in the creation of mood.' Wölfflin included the *St Peter's, Rome* painting by Panini to illustrate the mood of Baroque architecture in *Renaissance und Barock* (1888).

Five Traits of Mood in Formalism

1. Mood from Stimmung
The concept of mood when understood from the German word *Stimmung* is much more than a temporary state of mind. Tracing its philological origins opens mood to the harmonious bond capable of joining disparate elements: objective and subjective, factual and psychological, formal and ephemeral, man and environment.

2. Mood as motivation of formalism
The concept of mood, especially in relationship to the psychology of perception, is deeply embedded in the foundation of formalism: so much so that it is impossible to discuss formalism without alluding to it. Furthermore, the English translation 'mood' in the seminal text of Wölfflin and Riegl cannot fully describe the more expansive meaning of *Stimmung* from the native German text.

3. Transmitting mood through synaesthesia
Mood has the ability to negotiate between the objective and subjective due to synaesthesia. The stimulation of one sense triggers other senses and allows *Stimmung* to transition from its conception in music, to mathematics, to geometry, light, colour, environment and psyche. Recognising form as a possible medium for synaesthesia positions architecture as a vehicle for tuning mood.

4. Mood for deciphering architecture without canon
Mood is a critical vehicle to assess architecture without canon and in extension to design without canon. The current state of architecture operates largely in the vacuum of a contemporary canon due to the futility of universal language in a multicultural global society. Mood is a more immediate and universal approach for design via the psychology of perception.

5. Figuring Mood
Increased formal complexity and figuration affords the opportunity for heightened perception of mood through its capacity to capture and curate incorporeal elements of its environment, including light, shadow, colour, sound and atmosphere. Ultimately, through disfiguration, form moves toward the incorporeal itself.

Stimmung (Mood) and *Einfühlung* (Empathy)

Mood or *Stimmung* when understood in the full philological spectrum incorporates a complex interplay from the rational, numerical or mental comprehension to a subjective or emotional reception of a larger environment, atmosphere and connection to the cosmos. In this light, it is interesting to draw attention to the role of *Stimmung* in formalism, often overlooked as an integral concept in its foundation by Heinrich Wölfflin and Alois Riegl.

Wölfflin and Riegl recognised the value of the quickly developing scientific field of psychology in the late 19th century as a fertile ground for a more consequential approach to art history. Their approach sought to identify and tie formal attributes of representation to optical and tactile perception. Through the psychology of perception, considered universal, they could make a case for associating architecture with particular 'moods of the age', major aspects of which are experienced in dualities such as thinking and feeling but also art and science.[7]

Wölfflin's dissertation, *Prolegomena to a Psychology of Architecture* (1886), takes influence from Robert Vischer's (1847–1933) Empathy Theory (*Einfühlung*). Vischer promoted the notion that observers of art involuntarily transfer their own emotional moods to objects, finding resemblances between external things and our own mental states, experiences, sensations, moods, emotions and passions.[8] Wölfflin's first line of inquiry reads: 'The observations that follow concern a question that seems to me an altogether remarkable one: "How is it possible that architectural forms are able to express an emotion or a mood [*Stimmung*]?"'[9] Wölfflin asserts that the experience of architecture goes beyond pure geometric terms to 'massive forms'. Form communicates through moods or great 'vital feelings' that presuppose a constant stable body condition. Expression of mood is through posture and organisational composition of parts common to both architecture and the human body part-to-whole.

Analogous to Sigmund Freud's (1856–1939) experimental psychology, Wölfflin sought out a pathological or 'degenerate' architectural style to 'psychoanalyse' for his second book *Renaissance und Barock* (1888). Of the Baroque, Wölfflin wrote: 'It has become customary to use the term Baroque to describe the style into which the Renaissance resolved itself or, as it is more commonly expressed, into which the Renaissance degenerated.'[10] The seemingly idiosyncratic period of architecture after the Renaissance known as the Baroque had resisted systematic classification; however, there were important reasons for a more rigorous examination of the Baroque at the turn of the 20th century. The rise of industrialisation demanded an architectural response to scale outside of classical ideals of beauty. In addition, Germany's acquisition of the 2nd-century-BC Pergamon Altar in 1901 brought attention to the Hellenistic style with similar tendencies to the Baroque including more aggressive figuration and monumental scale. Finally, there was a general need for art history to expand its focus toward the contemporary.[11]

Even without a unifying canon, Baroque architecture could not elude assessment through the psychology of perception. The single most distinguishable characteristic of the Baroque mood is what Wölfflin deemed its 'painterly' quality, as opposed to the 'linear' quality of the Renaissance. For Wölfflin, the painterly effect is dependent on the theatrical manipulation of light and shadow, chiaroscuro: 'It is the Baroque that first uses light as an essential element in the creation of mood.'[12] Baroque architecture borrows its techniques for creating mood from painting, thus operating outside of the expected perception of architecture and its more classical state or mood. For the Renaissance mood, Wölfflin extols characteristics associated with the classical interpretation of *Stimmung* including elegant, harmonious, graceful, light, self-contained, individualistic, tectonic, calm, beautiful, uniform, perfect, born easily, free, complete, broad, pleasing, satisfactory, heavenly, content, slow, quiet, enduring and fulfilled. Quite opposite, Baroque mood is described as broad, massive, heavy, dissonant, amorphous, formless, imprisoned, un-evolved, incomplete, immediate, intimidating, overwhelming, exciting, ecstatic, intoxicating, momentary, desolating, anticipating, dissatisfactory, restless, tense. The break with the Renaissance canon is further emphasised throughout *Renaissance und Barock* by a continual comparison with and reference to the classic part-to-whole relationship established by Alberti and the dissolution of this rule by the Baroque.

Stimmung (Mood) and *Kunstwollen* (Will to Art)

Although grouped together as authors of the formalist project, both Alois Riegl and Heinrich Wölfflin held different attitudes toward the role mood played. Riegl staged the trajectory of man's 'will to art' (*Kunstwollen*) in a series of evolutionary steps comparable to the evolution of perception from child to adult. Children first develop an ability to see shape and profile through a haptic or close view, and then as they grow older are able to perceive more complex form through shadows, light and depth, building figural relationships through the optic or far view. Tied to this perceptual evolution, Riegl proposed three stages of human relationship with the world: will (*der Wille*), feeling (*die Empfindung*) and attention (*die Aufmerksamkeit*). Riegl's first stage, will, was embodied in art as man's triumphant (domination and subordination) conquest over a hostile environment epitomised in the rudimentary forms of Egyptian art. More important to our discussion of mood, the secondary stage of morphological growth was characterised by emotion or feeling. At this stage, nature is no longer considered an obstacle to overcome. Rather than a desire to dominate, the second stage, feeling, elicits a more complex emotional response informing Riegl's assessment of the Baroque: 'The exaggerated shapes and positions of Roman Baroque art are understood by Riegl to be the result of *feeling* or emotion breaking through the domination of the *will*.'[13] As a critical departure from Wölfflin, who positioned the Baroque as binary opposite (pathologically opposed) to the classical canon of beauty, Riegl positions the Baroque as evolutionarily more complex than the Renaissance both in mood and form. Erwin Panofsky, a champion of Riegl, further elaborates: 'The Baroque is not the decline, let alone the end of what we call the Renaissance era. It is in reality the second great climax of this great period and, at the same time, the beginning of a fourth era, which may be called "Modern" with a capital M.'[14]

Arabesque column capital, miniature painting and mural ornaments from Alois Riegl, *Problems of Style*, 1893

top, bottom left and right: Influenced by Impressionism, Riegl saw mood or *Stimmung* as the inevitable formal and aesthetic response for artistic engagement of nature and here draws comparison to ornament that acquires soft outlines, physical roundness, in short: life. The intricacy of the arabesque ornament captures the air between it (the figure and the object) and its environment.

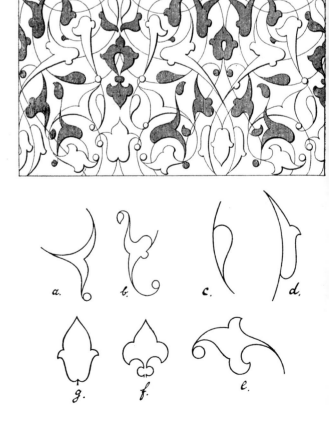

Children first develop an ability to see shape and profile through a haptic or close view, and then as they grow older are able to perceive more complex form through shadows, light and depth, building figural relationships through the optic or far view.

Andrew Saunders Architecture + Design with Gary Polk, Refracted Object Aggregation and Ruled Geometry of Refracted Light Simulation, 2015

As a contemporary projection of Heinrich Wölffin's painterly lighting effects of Baroque architecture, computational simulation of light refraction is used to generate geometric deflection of straight-line light ray vectors when passing obliquely through a medium or volume of varying density.

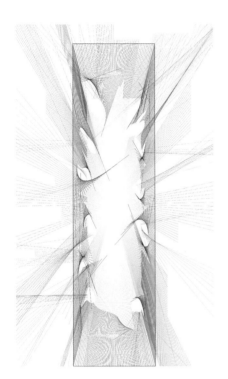

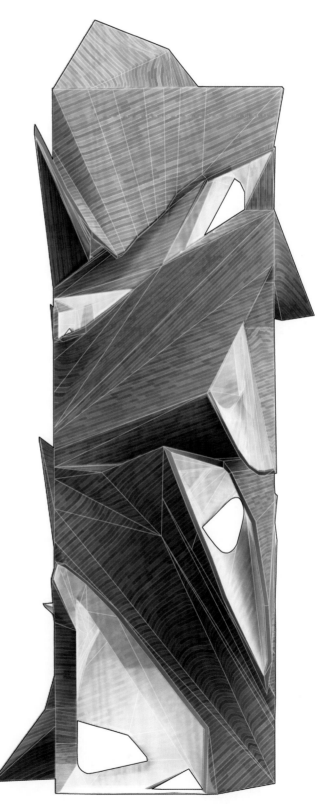

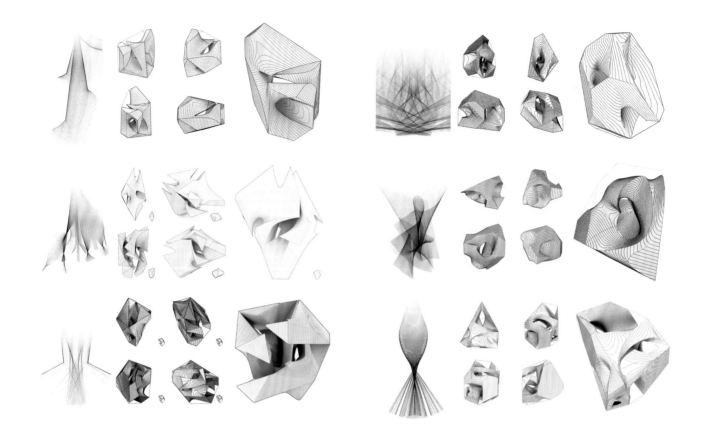

Yihui Gan, Gary Polk and Natasha Sanjaya,
Refracted Objects (Studio Andrew Saunders,
PennDesign, University of Pennsylvania),
2015

Chao Liu, Doug Breuer, Elsa Listiani,
Refracted Objects (Studio Andrew Saunders,
PennDesign, University of Pennsylvania),
2015

Formal research of figuration through ruled geometry of
refracted light simulation.

Stimmung is not tangible, it is not
an object or a figure, and no tactile,
haptic perception of it is conceivable.

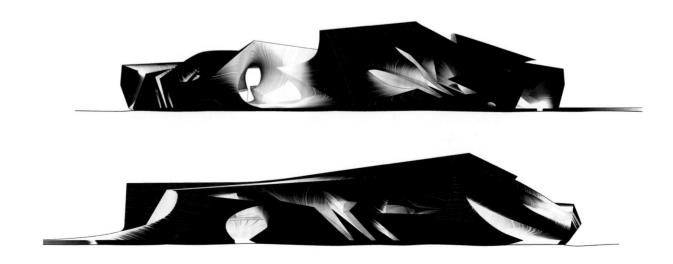

In his essay *Mood as the Content of Modern Art* (1889), Riegl ultimately positions mood or *Stimmung* as the inevitable formal and aesthetic response for artistic engagement of nature within an empirically modern scientific world of causality.[15] Moshe Barasch explains: '*Stimmung* is not tangible, it is not an object or a figure, and no tactile, haptic perception of it is conceivable. *Stimmung* necessarily requires optic perception or distant vision.'[16] Barasch makes clear the influence of impressionism quoting Riegl: 'hard things treated in the newer manner seem to acquire soft outlines, physical roundness, in short: life … Sometimes one imagines one sees the air between it (the figure and the object) and its environment. Thus the painter paints even the incorporeal.'

It is interesting to note how integral mood, so ephemeral and unable to be fully realised through pure figuration, was to the inception of formalism. The late 19th-century critics found their concepts for more primitive form, linear (Wölfflin) and haptic (Riegl), ideally suited to architecture as a medium and both found it increasingly difficult for the physicality of architecture to convincingly embody the more innovative formal complexity of painterly illusion. In the contemporary paradigm of architecture where advances in visualisation, simulation, fabrication and automation are all fuelled by digital technology, illusive affects once only obtainable in representation are now more easily embodied in the actuality of architecture. ∆

ary Polk, Refracted Objects
Studio Andrew Saunders, PennDesign,
niversity of Pennsylvania),
015

*elow and opposite bottom: Detail and full view:
*ggregations of volumetric spatial figures of
*ht refraction simulations are articulated using
iaroscuro effects with lighter tonal mapping at
eightened areas of refraction.

Notes
1. Heinrich Wölfflin, *Renaissance and Baroque* [*Renaissance und Baroque*, 1888], trans Kathrin Simon, Collins (London), 1964, p 77.
2. David Leatherbarrow, 'Atmospheric Conditions', in Henriette Steiner and Maximilian Sternberg (eds), *Phenomenologies of the City: Studies in the History and Philosophy of Architecture*, Routledge (London and New York), 2016, pp 85–100.
3. Leo Spitzer, *Classical and Christian Ideas of World Harmony: Prolegomena to an Interpretation of the Word 'Stimmung'*, Johns Hopkins Press (Baltimore, MD), 1963, pp 5 and 138.
4. Alberto Pérez-Gómez, *Attunement: Architectural Meaning after the Crisis of Modern Science*, MIT Press (Cambridge, MA), 2016, p 41.
5. Vitruvius, *Vitruvius: The Ten Books on Architecture*, Dover Publications, 1960, Book I, Chapter II, p 13.
6. Leon Battista Alberti, *On the Art of Building in Ten Books*, MIT Press (Cambridge, MA), 1991, Book VI, Chapter II, p 156.
7. Gevork Hartoonian, *The Mental Life of the Architectural Historian: Re-opening the Early Historiography of Modern Architecture*, Cambridge Scholars Publishing (Newcastle upon Tyne), 2010, pp 130–31.
8. Robert Vischer, 'On the Optical Sense of Form: A Contribution to Aesthetics', trans Harry Francis Mallgrave and Eleftherios Ikonomou, in *Empathy, Form, and Space: Problems in German Aesthetics, 1873–1893*, Getty Center for the History of Art (Chicago, IL), 1993, p 89.
9. Heinrich Wölfflin, 'Prolegomena to a Psychology of Architecture', trans Harry Francis Mallgrave and Eleftherios Ikonomou, in *Empathy, Form, and Space: Problems in German Aesthetics, 1873-1893*, Getty Center for the History of Art (Chicago, IL), 1993, p 149.
10. Wölfflin, *Renaissance and Baroque*, op cit, p 15.
11. Alina Payne, 'Beyond Kunstwollen', in Alois Riegl, *The Origins of Baroque Art in Rome*, Getty Research Institute (Los Angeles, CA), 2010, pp 1–9.
12. Wölfflin, *Renaissance and Baroque*, op cit, p 123.
13. Margaret Iverson, *Alois Riegl: Art History and Theory*, MIT Press (Cambridge, MA), 1993, p 95.
14. Erwin Panofsky, *What Is Baroque? Three Essays on Style*, MIT Press (Cambridge, MA), 1995, p 88.
15. Alois Riegl, 'Die Stimmung als Inhalt der modernen Kunst', in *Gesammelte Aufsätze*, Gebr. Mann Verlag (Berlin), 1995, p 28.
16. Moshe Barasch, *Theories of Art, 1: From Plato to Winckelmann*, Routledge (New York and London), 2000, pp 159–60.

Jason
Payne

Low Albedo

The Mathilde Project

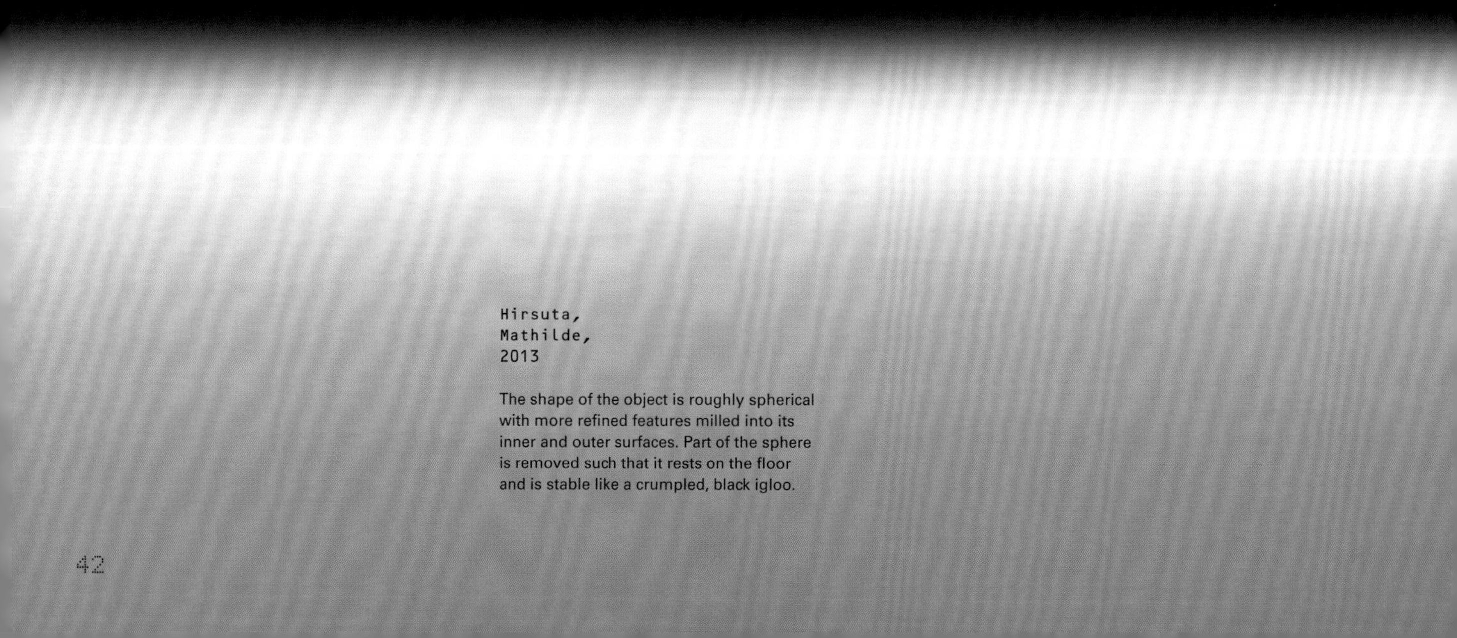

Hirsuta,
Mathilde,
2013

The shape of the object is roughly spherical
with more refined features milled into its
inner and outer surfaces. Part of the sphere
is removed such that it rests on the floor
and is stable like a crumpled, black igloo.

It is hard to imagine anything more darkly moody than a slow-rotating, ultra-black asteroid lurking in deep outer space. Los Angeles-based practice Hirsuta's recent Mathilde project is directly inspired by such an object, turning it inside out in an inversion of space and form. **Jason Payne**, principal of his practice, which combines a focus on materiality and sensual stimulation with an exploration of emerging construction technologies, describes it.

Asteroids are profoundly closed objects, their observation possible only from outside and from afar. In this way their relation to us on Earth is one of constant recession, a turning away, a deep ambivalence to our ever knowing them. But what if one were to let us in, to let us see it from the inside? Hirsuta's Mathilde project (2013) imagines asteroid 253 Mathilde turned outside-in, making space of the object. An impulse to construct a very strange and dark form, it initiates a new foray into the old problem of the subject–object relationship. Mathilde's affect and atmosphere, however, are something relatively unusual – and so then is its mood.

Of all the curious objects moving through our solar system, asteroid 253 Mathilde really *is* strange. Mathilde is a main-belt asteroid that circles the sun every four years between the orbits of Mars and Jupiter. Discovered in 1885 by Johann Palisa, little more than its existence was known before NASA's Near Earth Asteroid Rendezvous (NEAR) Shoemaker spacecraft flew by it on the 27 June 1997. In its description in five points below, each bears some relevance to architectural form.

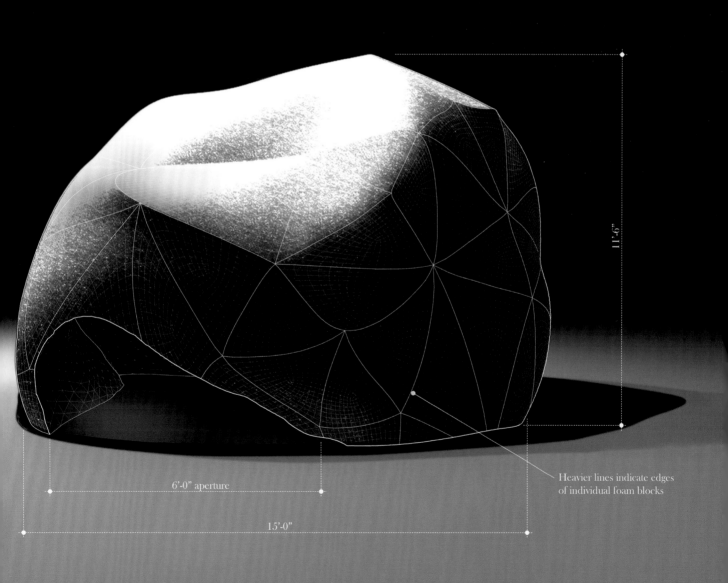

11'-6"

6'-0" aperture

15'-0"

Heavier lines indicate edges
of individual foam blocks

43

Mathilde is *Black*

Specifically, its albedo (the reflection coefficient, or brightness, of a surface) measures as low as virtually any known object or material, reflecting only 3 per cent of the Sun's light. Twice as dark as charcoal, Mathilde's elevational aspect is nearly that of space itself, making it extraordinarily difficult to see and photograph. Ambivalent, it would seem, to the traditional and dichotomous relationships of object to field, mass to volume, body to context. As it slowly rotates it presents a continually changing figure as its outer profile appears to slip away into the dark of space, making edges difficult to discern. A study in black, Mathilde presents real problems of representation for astrophysicists and architects alike, since each is more accustomed to objects with more pronounced optics. The definition of an object indifferent to legibility suggests that standard, disciplinary means of representation be questioned and may very well require the development of new methods of visualisation.

Mathilde is Compositionally and Structurally *Loose*

Discovery of its low density came as a surprise to NEAR scientists since a solid carbon asteroid of this size should measure twice its estimated weight. This qualifies Mathilde for inclusion in a special class of asteroids known as a 'rubble pile', a loosely packed bunch of smaller objects held tenuously together through gravity as well as a certain measure of luck, since the slightest bump could disperse the entire organisation. Current measurements give Mathilde a 50:50 ratio of solid to void, meaning that despite outward appearances it is as open as it is closed, and that there is indeed space within an asteroid. Here again we see an object rather ambivalent to conventional readings, hiding a voluminous interior beneath the thinnest cloak of dust and debris, feature and figure.

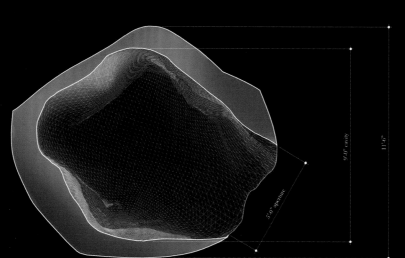

The surfaces inside and out are precisely figured and tight, while the structural logic itself is rather loose: blocks laid one beside the other rotating slowly upwards similar to a traditional dome composition. The ratio of mass to internal volume near 50:50 giving the impression of neither object nor space, but both, ambivalently.

Mathilde is *Monolithic*

Most objects of study in the world are material composites, and this is true of astrophysical bodies as well. Planets, stars, comets and even most other asteroids are made up of compound organisations, but Mathilde is thought to be only carbon through and through. Evidence of this comes from the fact that Mathilde is not only black, but uniformly black even across the slopes of its large craters. It represents a 'pristine sample of the primitive building blocks of the larger planets'[1] – a primitive hut in the terms of our own discipline – suggesting formal complexity without material complication.

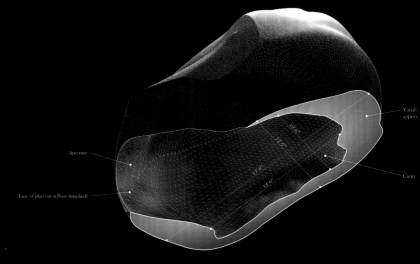

Monolithicity is achieved through the use of a single-material, high-density milled foam. The outer surface of the foam is no different to the mass within; if there is any notion of 'skin' at all it is one of pure geometry. The entire object is black, through and through. Unlike form in any other colour, this one resists even the most ardent attempt at objectification by the subject – or at least shrugs it off.

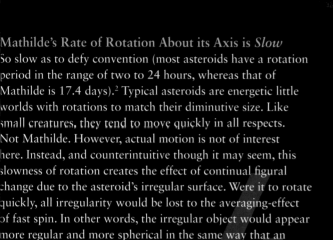

Unlike a regular igloo, all aspects of this object cannot be derived from a single station point, requiring the viewer to move about the perimeter even prior to going inside.

Mathilde's Rate of Rotation About its Axis is *Slow*

So slow as to defy convention (most asteroids have a rotation period in the range of two to 24 hours, whereas that of Mathilde is 17.4 days).[2] Typical asteroids are energetic little worlds with rotations to match their diminutive size. Like small creatures, they tend to move quickly in all respects. Not Mathilde. However, actual motion is not of interest here. Instead, and counterintuitive though it may seem, this slowness of rotation creates the effect of continual figural change due to the asteroid's irregular surface. Were it to rotate quickly, all irregularity would be lost to the averaging-effect of fast spin. In other words, the irregular object would appear more regular and more spherical in the same way that an apple, spun fast, looks more like a ball.

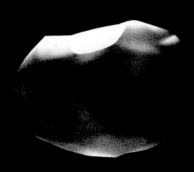

Mathilde is *Geometrically Ambivalent*

Because it is neither spherical nor is it *not* spherical. The most famous bodies in the solar system are spherical, while many lesser objects are highly irregular. Mathilde is neither. From afar it looks generally round, but upon close reading is found to have a surface so tortured by impact craters as to push it towards irregularity. Moreover, the size and number of craters for an asteroid of this size and composition shocked NEAR observers: '[A]t first glance there are more huge craters than there is asteroid.'[3] Again a reference to Mathilde's ambivalence towards solid and void, inside and outside. For our purposes, this implies an 'anexact' geometry of sorts, neither exact nor inexact, capable of defining a thing that hovers between Platonic ideal and more prosaic organisations of real matter, something nearly spherical, but not really. In this way, Mathilde's moody and difficult estrangement from our intrusive impulse for colonisation through measurement remains intact.

A Note on Mood

In this age of genres, only some of which are defined by mood, Hirsuta's ideas and the work described here may be closer to something like 'goth'. If so, what do this darkening of mood and the Gothic more generally have to do with architecture? In popular music, Goth emerged to a significant degree from heavy metal, a form of music that, however groundbreaking in its origins, came to suffer from the hegemony of formulaic repetition, not unlike what many of us see in the architectural 'parametricism' of today. Blind expertise reiterated cannot support endless fascination or even sustained interest, and soon gives way to boredom. For all its formal promise, material ambition and technical prowess, it would appear that parametricism has no mood. The darkening described above, despite its reliance upon similar geometrical and material aspirations, is a 'moodiness' rather than a 'moodlessness'. With the insistence of the Mathilde project upon 'objecthood' over field, however shy this object may be, the occult(ed) status of the object in architecture might once more be questioned. ◬

Notes
1. See Helen Worth, 'Asteroid Mathilde Reveals Her Dark Past', press release, 30 June 1997: www.nasa.gov/home/hqnews/1997/97-147.txt.
2. See Kenneth R Lang, '2. Asteroids and Meteorites: Size, Color, and Spin', NASA's Cosmos, 2003: ase.tufts.edu/cosmos/view_chapter.asp?id=15&page=3.
3. Joseph Veverka of Cornell University, leader of the NEAR mission's imaging science team, quoted in Worth, *op cit*.

An Interview with Wolf D Prix of Coop Himmelb(l)au

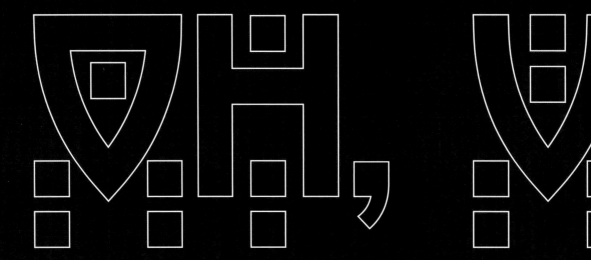

Vienna-based Coop Himmelb(l)au
has been making adrenaline-fuelled
contributions to the architectural scene
ever since its foundation in 1968 by
Wolf D Prix, Helmut Swiczinsky and
Michael Holzer. In discussion with
Guest-Editor **Matias del Campo**, Prix
looks back over almost four decades
of the firm's existence. Among
other things, he reflects on its early
investigations into space-modifying
feedback systems in response to users'
heartbeats, and on later experiments
in initiating design with eyes closed
in order to channel emotional impact
rather than pure formal logic.

Vienna in 1969 must have been a spectacular place to be. Something happened there, something strange, something provocative, something beautiful; as if the suppressed creativity of 40 years was compressed beyond the critical mass and wildly detonated in a plethora of artistic achievements. Rubbing against its conservative society, still covered in the grey dust of the postwar era and still mourning (in a subconscious layer) the loss of its empire, the city was suddenly – almost violently – confronted with a young generation of artists eager to embark on the discovery of the new, and enthusiastically embracing aspects of the visionary. Actionism was the dernier cri, and artists such as Hermann Nitsch, Otto Mühl and Günter Brus formed the spearhead of this highly provocative movement.

Vienna's architectural community at this time turned out to be a particularly fertile ground for the exploration of new and radical ideas about the formation of a project, the definition of space and the nature of architecture. The event itself became part of the architectural oeuvre. Collaboratives and cooperations formed almost instantly around the legendary 'club seminar' of Günther Feuerstein,[1] who at the time was teaching at the Technical University in Vienna, to confront students with material that was rarely published in German-speaking countries. Groups such as Zünd-Up, Missing Link, Haus-Rucker-Co, Salz der Erde and, of course, Coop Himmelb(l)au framed this moment in time, which was fittingly named the 'Austrian Phenomenon'.[2]

Günter Brus, Vienna Walk, 1965

In Vienna of the late 1960s, still trapped in a postwar depression, the hot friction between the arts and society provoked actionism and an unsatiable desire for a visionary perspective.

The Grand Utopian Project

Starting in 1968, Coop Himmelb(l)au developed an interest in feedback systems that allowed the manipulation of a space in response to the user's mood. Wolf D Prix, the cofounder of Coop Himmelb(l)au, explains the origin of some of the group's early installations: 'The grand utopian project "Himmelblaue Kreislaufstadt" was an urban structure where each inhabitant was able to project his heartbeat, his brain activity and his motion patterns on to large public spaces. In the best case, the heartbeat of a million inhabitants could be seen or heard simultaneously.' This initial project spawned a series of actions and interventions that utilised the response of the human body to sensorial stimulation and vice versa to manipulate the formation of space. Projects like Face Space – Soul Flipper, the White Suit and Astro Balloon (all created in Vienna in 1969) not only represent early examples of interactive architecture, they also address the problem of an intensified relationship between the architectural device and the emotional state of the inhabitant.

Coop Himmelb(l)au,
Face Space – Soul Flipper,
1969

above and below: The Soul Flipper project harnessed the responses of the human body to sensorial stimulation to manipulate the formation of space.

Coop Himmelb(l)au,
The White Suit,
1969

Coop Himmelb(l)au's interest in the feedback between technological devices and the user spawned projects like Face Space – Soul Flipper, the White Suit and Astro Balloon (all Vienna 1969). These can be considered prototypes of interactive environments, exploring the relationship between the architectural device and the emotional state of the inhabitant.

The projects were primarily documented with the methods established by the actionists, with the artefact, the reliquary of the action, devised by excellent photography, drawings, sketches, collages, filming material, letters, press clippings and other archival material. These well-curated artefacts formed the main body of the forensic remains of Coop Himmelb(l)au's actions of the late 1960s. But despite the group's insistence on the importance of the subject, there is no record of how the 'realisation' of these works actually took place. After all, these were not just buildings or structures to inhabit, but responsive apparatuses that needed an individual with sentiments and sensory organs to be complete. Coop Himmelb(l)au did, however, understand the importance of documenting the group's work through photography, and often used human models to stage their installations.[3] In doing so, the installations level the field between the object of architecture and the object of the human body, allowing the architecture to enter into a conversation on equal terms. Interactivity in the best sense of the word.

The Heartbeat as Obsession

A recurring aspect of Coop Himmelb(l)au's early installations is the obsession with the heartbeat. Projects such as Astro Balloon, Himmelblaue Kreislaufstadt (Vienna, 1968) and Hard Space (Schwechat, 1970) focus on the heartbeat as a means of expression or a responsive generator of form. Astro Balloon, which was revisited in 2008 for the Venice Architecture Biennale, is as much sensor and technical object as it is architectural environment – calibrated to respond to the heartbeat of the occupant, and to change, transform and mutate in various colourful ways in accordance with the flux of the pulsation recorded by its sensorial system. The intimate relationship and feedback between sensorial stimulation of the human body and the technological devices that respond to the user's mood are interrogated and celebrated. In a way, Coop Himmelb(l)au were here exploring the architectural equivalent to Jimmy Hendrix's discovery of feedback as a virtuous musical technique, rather than an annoyance to be avoided. The violent, overwhelming sublime property of thundering, screaming loud feedback forms a bodily experience beyond listening to a melody. Hard Space might be the most radical approach to this idea.

Coop Himmelb(l)au,
Astro Balloon,
1969

above and right:
The handles underneath the spherical helmet were
outfitted with sensors able to pick up the heartbeat
of the user. The signal was then transformed into
audiovisual stimuli, creating a feedback loop between
the user and the environment.

Somewhere
between ignition and the
myriad of dirt particles
settling back on the ground,
a highly intricate, animated
space was established
for a brief moment
in time

In this project, sensors picked up the heartbeats of the
members of the group, which triggered detonators that created
60 explosions in the landscape. The cloud of dust created in
an instant an animated and highly complex spatial entity that
disappeared almost as quickly as it emerged.

Prix states that: 'It would be an error to believe that atmosphere (*Stimmung*) or ephemeral effects were part of our interest in our early projects.' The constitutive force in the projects was not defined by the atmosphere or mood of the object itself, but rather through the properties induced by the user, the inhabitant. Simply put: the inhabitant is in a mood. These operations can be described as a feedback loop that operates beyond the description of the project as a bundle of qualities. In fact, it rather responds to a question oscillating between two speculative poles: one being the real and the sensual, the other posing inquiries about the object and its qualities.[4]

Hard Space and Soft Space (Vienna, 1970) – yet another duality – thus describe in a radical fashion the manifestation of instantaneously generated spatial conditions. Technically speaking, in the Hard Space project the hearts of the Coop Himmelb(l)au group members were wired to a monitor, and the electrical sparks triggered by the beats detonated 60 explosive charges across the Schwechat landscape, unleashing architectural mayhem on a stone quarry in this Viennese suburb famous for its beer brewery and a rather unimpressive airport. Somewhere between ignition and the myriad of dirt particles settling back on the ground, a highly intricate, animated space was established for a brief moment in time; the manifestation of a rapidly emerging and decaying feedback system that does not trust a design strategy that relies solely on the designer's will,[5] but also takes into account aspects of coincidence and the nature of external forces such as wind and gravity.

Open House: *Entwurf* is not Design

The German word '*Entwurf*' is a hard nut to crack. It means much more than its primary English translation, 'design', would suggest. '*Entfernen*', '*Entsinnen*', '*Entfachen*' and '*Entreissen*', like '*Entwerfen*' are all verbs based on activities, and all possess a much wider set of cultural meanings than any attempt to translate them would reveal. Maybe German is not as precise a language as it is usually attributed to be after all, its vocabulary suggestive of manifold connotations. And the nominalisation of terms does not make the entire affair any easier to grasp. In the late 1970s, Coop Himmelb(l)au was pondering the meaning of the term *Entwurf*, which incorporates '*wurf*', '*werfen*' – 'to throw': 'We started analysing the nature of architectural design methodologies. We were eager to change architecture now, immediately and radically. It seemed obvious to change the most sensible steps in the design process in order to transform the design strategy to discover new forms of architecture.'

If the Hard Space intervention was the manifestation of an ephemeral spatial condition based on action and feedback, then the Open House (Malibu, California, 1983) was another radical distant cousin throwing (*werfen*) historical ballast overboard and completely breaking with the conventions of architectural design. Coop Himmelb(l)au's approach here could not have been more opposed to the then-common Postmodern methods like the ubiquitous referencing of historical forms, and the quasi-religious belief that if you follow the teachings of Vitruvius, Palladio or Alberti, all will be good:[6]

Coop Himmelb(l)au,
Open House,
Malibu, California,
1983

above top:
The initial sketch of the Open House, drawn on tracing paper with eyes shut, formed the basis for the entire design. The intuitive motion of the hand served as a seismograph for the emotions the building would evoke.

above:
The model mirrors in a very accurate fashion the nature of the spontaneous, automatic first drawing.

below:
The structural engineer of the Open House, Wolfdietrich Ziesel, once described it as a crossbreed between a bridge and aeroplane. The whole building rests on only two points, and is held in place by the tension between static and dynamic moments that can be sensed even at the model scale.

The rigid, computational design methods were not yet invented around the time we designed the Open House. Our analysis of the term *Entwurf* resulted in our conviction that all rational predicaments have to be excluded from the design process in order to emancipate the architectural space. The first sketch, which formed the basis for the entire design, was drawn with our eyes closed, and the hand served as a seismograph, which allowed the inscription of all the emotions that the building would evoke. It was not the details that were important at that moment, but the radiance of light and shadows, brightness and darkness, height and width, whiteness and vaulting, the view and the air. The flow of energy in the drawing is translated into concrete form and structure. The building – resting on two points and taut – almost floats.

he sketch itself bears the marks of the violent struggle to hrow' the design on the paper. A piece of Aquafix, the common rafting paper still in use today, is tattered, ripped on both ends. accommodates the rather small drawing, which could be a plan, a section, or a perspective, but in fact is all of it at once, or othing of it at all. There is an uncanny power to it, as if the thing n itself evokes the possible moods in the strange, contorted and ndivided space it proposes. The rigour with which the original rawing was translated into a fully fledged building project certain steel parts were produced at 1:1 scale) is admirable, and emands deep respect. The entire history of the project to this day ould probably make an entertaining book, even though the last hapter is certainly not yet written.

Under closer examination, the artistic technique of the Open House project in itself resembles two of art history's most celebrated movements and their methods: the Dadaist desire to harness the power of the accidental, and the insight of German Romanticism as to the value of emotional response as an artistic form of expression. With all of this in mind, it is necessary to understand that Coop Himmelb(l)au's point is not that the object itself possesses mood, but rather that architecture possesses the ability to negotiate between light and shadow, brightness and darkness, height and width, the view and the air, and its occupants. All of which meet on a level plane field that allows for multiple interactions, ultimately perceived as a possible mood. Wolf D Prix's response to the question as to whether there is a moody architecture: 'There is no moody architecture, only moody architects.'

Vienna in 2016 must be a spectacular place to be. Something is happening there, something strange, something provocative, something beautiful. Zeitgeist is most certainly a force to be reckoned with when it comes to progress in the architectural discipline – the longing for the radically new, the desire to shrug the dust of history off the shoulders, the will to take a risk. All of this remains present in the current work of Coop Himmelb(l)au. Hard Space and Open House can be considered prototypes of radical design ambitions, blueprints of an insatiable desire for a change in the ever-so-slowly evolving discipline of architecture. Over the years, they have spawned an entire universe of unconventional spatial solutions, described so inimitably as jumping whales, warm bellies, hot heads, crystals and clouds. Coop Himmelb(l)au continues to overtake on the highway without looking in the rear mirror, its work still an architecture of the adrenaline rush. ⌀

This interview is the result of email correspondence between the author and Wolf D Prix during the spring of 2016, and a face-to-face meeting in May at the opening of the Venice Architecture Biennale.

Notes
1. See also Günther Feuerstein, *Visionäre Architektur in Wien 1958–1988*, Ernst, Wilhelm und Sohn (Vienna), 1988.
2. Peter Cook, *Experimental Architecture*, Universe Books (New York), 1970, p 12.
3. Victoria Bugge Øye and Another Space, 'Nicht Realisiert: In Search of Lost Experience', Another Space, Copenhagen, 28 September–19 October 2014: http://anotherspace.dk/2012-2014/nicht-realisiert-in-search-of-lost-experience/.
4. Graham Harman, *Weird Realism: Lovecraft and Philosophy*, Zero Books (Winchester and Washington DC), 2012, p 4.
5: For a closer examination of the topic of will and imagination, see Arthur Schopenhauer, *The World as Will and Representation*, Brockhaus (Leipzig), 1844 (2nd expanded edn).
6: See also Coop Himmelb(l)au, *Architecture Must Blaze*, Institut für Gebäudelehre der TU Graz (Graz), 1980.

Coop Himmelb(l)au,
Astro Balloon,
11th Venice Architecture Biennale,
2008

The small-scale Astro Balloon installation of 1969 revisited at a much larger scale in 2008. This iteration of the project comes much closer to the original intention not only of the Astro Balloon, but to the entire family of pneumatic installations designed by Coop Himmelb(l)au in the late 1960s and early 1970s.

Moody Objects

Ore Fashion Stores and Blocks

The leading figures of Modernism instilled a fear of ornament as something unclean and even criminal. Guest-Editor **Matias del Campo** calls for us to leave behind this phobia and engage anew with ornament for the purposes of generating mood and atmosphere. Here he describes two recent projects by SPAN, the Vienna-based architectural practice he cofounded with Sandra Manninger, which explore alternatives to the usual aesthetic canons by addressing classic architectural problems in bold new ways.

Adolf Loos was enormously successful in inducing fear of articulation in the architectural discipline. In his famous *Streitschrift* 'Ornament and Crime', which he first presented as a lecture in Vienna in 1910, he fiercely condemned the decor of buildings as a 'waste of time and resources',[1] his main argument being that the laborious manual production of ornamentation stole the lifetimes away of the craftsmen involved in its production. In his American Bar (1908), in the same city, what was lost in designed ornamentation was replaced by the visually rich qualities of stone striations, polished brass and undulating architectural garments. His dismissal of any form of spatial articulation soon became quickly at hand in any architectural discussion of the period, and was to be a huge influence for modern icons such as Mies van der Rohe and Le Corbusier who considered 'Ornament and Crime' a 'Homeric cleansing' of architecture.

But what if we leave behind the fear of ornament? What if we intentionally work with aspects of mood and atmosphere: chromatic effects, dissolved walls, flickering ceilings, flirting symmetries, grumpy illuminations, happy floors, fickle columns and awe-inspiring naves?

Philosophy professor Graham Harman's book *Weird Realism: Lovecraft and Philosophy* (2012)[2] scrutinises the Lovecraftian literary universe of weird objects, fear-inducing meteorites, sailor-swallowing corners, ancient arctic beings and alien voices vomited by humans – all of which evoke atmospheres of horror, the uncanny and unfamiliar. But at the same time, these deformations, or speculations on the nature of objects allow for specific architectural applications: the unshelving and repositioning of common features such as arches, columns and domes that are recognisable but still different.

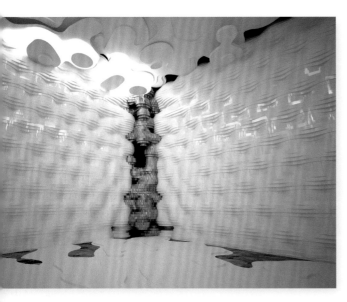

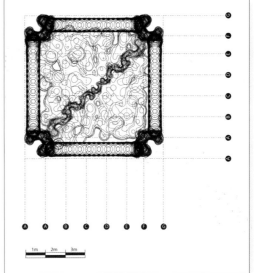

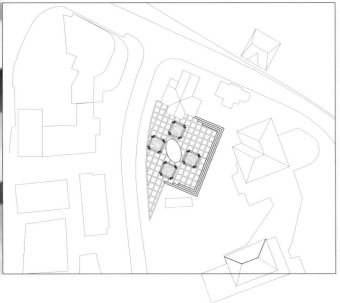

SPAN (Matias del Campo and Sandra Manninger), Ore Fashion Stores, Shanghai, 2015

opposite: The four concrete 3D-printed pavilions form a porous *carré*, loosely shaped like a rectangular square. The proposal is situated next to the Bund waterfront in Shanghai, the square dominated by a centrally positioned oval water basin.

top left: Ore specifically addresses the disciplinary problem of the corner in a contemporary fashion.

right: The plan of the Ore project oscillates between rigorous walls and sloppy corners, an undulating diagonal division serving as a divider between the two shops within each cube.

bottom left: The siteplan reveals the relationship between the four cubes and the fountain. The project produces its own contextualisation by occupying the square instead of adapting to the edges of the existing space.

ABoxVSShape forms a series of
vertical and horizontal strands that
are further subdivided to form
fenestrations, niches, pilasters,
mouldings and mullions.

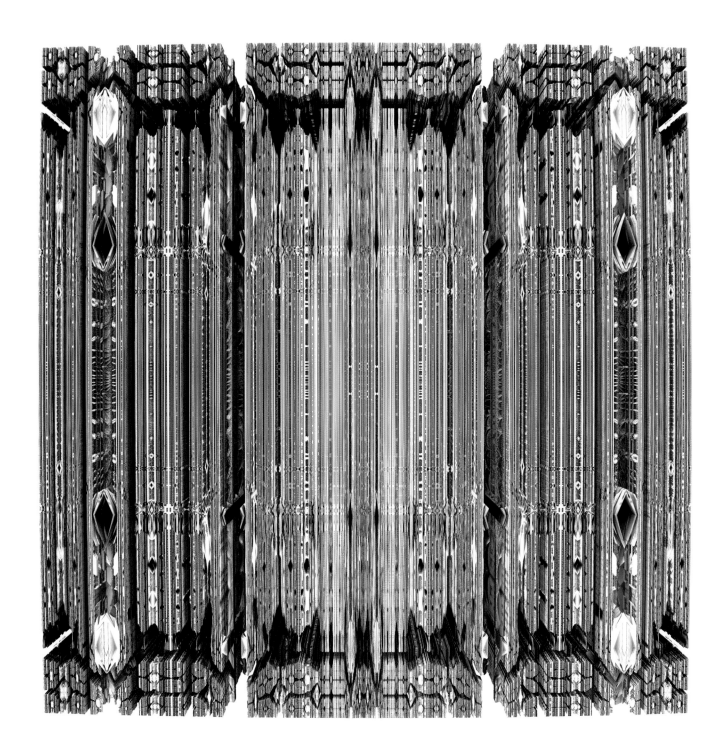

Blocks represents a primordial
exploration into the nature of
recursive elements in architecture
such as joints, columns and arches.

SPAN's Ore Fashion Stores and Blocks projects (both 2016) move away from digital design explicated purely by its technological qualities, abandoning the emphasis on the tool over the cultural potentialities, the material over the symbolic, and the utilitarian over the philosophical. Rather, they embrace the possibility of a posthuman design condition in which the raw, the coarse, the chiaroscuro of automated figurations, the fine-grained and the qualities of spatial articulation are embraced as a disciplinary problem.

Ore was commissioned for the 2016 Shanghai Fashion Week as a series of temporary shops for four exclusive brands specialising in the sale of 3D-printed clothing. Each of the four cubes holds two retail spaces. This division of each cube into two compartments is defined by an undulating diagonal wall that acts as a shelf and display, its convex/concave motion creating squinting niches that protrude into both of the retail spaces. The project approaches the primordial architectural problem of the corner by parsing the order and seducing it to become raw, its rough nature softened by the application of gold foil. The four shopping pavilions form an intimate relationship – a porous open-air *carré* used for fashion shows, theatrical productions, lectures and more.

Blocks represents a primordial exploration into the nature of recursive elements in architecture such as joints, columns and arches. The project can be seen in the tradition of the abstract machine. SPAN has utilised abstract machines as the point of origin for a series of projects that represent a collection of possible architectures and are as much plan, section and perspective as they are detail, house or urban block. These vague denominations form the basis for the relationship between all of these objects. Blocks functions outside distinct contextualisations, whether historical or urban, instead embracing an abstract niche within the architectural canon. The scale-less nature and recursive properties of things such as Blocks are interrogated intensively for their ability to fuse the concept with the sensation, their contingencies proposing explicit architectural objects.

Both Ore and Blocks operate between autonomous objects and disciplinary provocations. They address specific architectural problems such as turning the corner, the negotiation of mass, void and subdivision, and the spatial richness produced by arches, pillars, chimneys, niches, cornices and crests, which positions them amidst the familiar and the strange. The qualities of defamiliarisation and the weird create opportunities to speculate about alternative aesthetical canons. The only reason why any object can be considered strange, weird or even ugly is because it challenges preconceived, culturally imprinted notions of beauty. However, removing these shackles activates alternative ways to explore other aesthetic conditions and an open discussion of how design can evoke a response – and not necessarily in a human observer after all. ◬

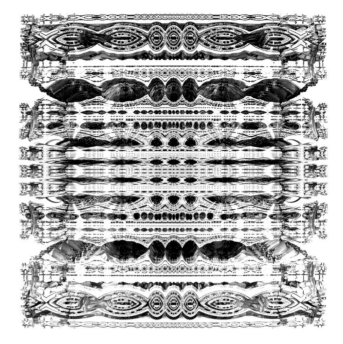

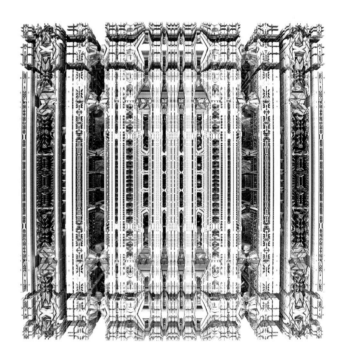

top: The Blocks series explores variations of disciplinary questions through algorithmic modelling: arches, bases, fluting, apertures and stacked layers of porous masses.

bottom: The combination of familiar architectural entities such as block, grid and frame with uncanny moments of unprecision and vague figuration serve as a base for the speculative nature of the project.

Notes
Adolf Loos, 'Ornament und Verbrechen', *Cahiers d'aujourd'hui*, 5, 1915, p 34.
Graham Harman, *Weird Realism: Lovecraft and Philosophy*, Zero Books
(Winchester and Washington DC), 2012.

Michael Young

The Affects of Realism

Or the Estrangement of the Background

Gustave Courbet, *The Stone Breakers*, 1849

The paintings of Courbet were a direct challenge on multiple levels to the conventions of the mid-century French Academies. They were everyday in content, yet scaled to a grand historical narrative, composed in abstract rhythms of alignments not balanced stable hierarchies, and painted in a rough texture that revealed the pigment and brush stroke in a manner rarely seen before.

Affect is not just about mood and fantasy; at its best, it is an aesthetic provocation that can generate a profound questioning of the nature of reality. The 19th-century Realist writers and artists understood this – and its political implications – well. After examining the theme with reference to the writings of an international array of cultural critics, architect **Michael Young** – cofounder with Kutan Ayata of the New York-based studio Young & Ayata – presents a project by his firm that is subtly designed to trigger affective sensations of defamiliarisation.

In Flaubert and Courbet we see an attack on these familiar structures of producing and interpreting meaning. The resulting void was filled with a new emphasis on the sensations of the body, or in other words, affect.

Affects revolve around embodied experiences of moods and sensations. Realism, on the other hand, deals with objects that exist outside of us. It describes the everyday world, often with the attitude of reportage. It should thus seem a bit strange to not only link the two topics, but to further suggest that in their modern condition affect and realism were born together in the 19th century. Yet this is exactly the thesis put forward by Fredric Jameson in his recent book *The Antinomies of Realism*. Jameson locates the emergence of the modern understanding of affect in the novels of Gustave Flaubert, Émile Zola and Leo Tolstoy, in other words from realism in literature.[1] These writers were able to shift the aesthetics of literature from a recitation of past events towards an activation of the body's senses engaged in a heightened experience of the real.

It is important for an architecture of the 21st century that wishes to engage the affective to remember these roots. This historical link is interesting not for offering a former expression as precedent, but for suggesting that the most intense affects are not those that produce a distance from reality through fantasy, but those that spring from an estrangement of realism; the possibility that the real can be other than we commonly assume.

Before we go further, there are three terms on the table that need to be explicated: 'sensation', 'affect' and 'realism'. For the following discussion they shall be defined as follows: Sensation pertains to the sensory responses of the body; it is differentiated from perception in that it is more reflexive than reflective, more tied to the body's reactions than to conscious intellectual reflection. Affect shall be used to describe the states of shifting subjectivity in relation to sensation. Affects are different from emotions. As argued by Jameson, affect resists the reduction to the nominal that emotion entails.[2] It is difficult to describe affective states as happy, sad, angry or jealous. It is likely that the affective is mixed, or more often just unnamable. Realism refers to an aesthetic stance. It should not be mistaken with 'reality' as an ontological argument pertaining to what does or does not exist. Instead, realism is an aesthetic argument that constantly shows reality to be a mediated construct. It provokes tensions between reality and its representation.

The Rise of the Everyday
Most discussions regarding realism find it arising first in the middle of the 19th century within the literature of Gustave Flaubert and the paintings of Gustave Courbet. The two Gustaves share commonalities beyond their given name and nationality. In their respective mediums, there is a new focus on the everyday as the content of their work. For instance, the adultery of a farmer's daughter in Flaubert's *Madame Bovary* (1856) or a common act of physical labour in Courbet's *The Stone Breakers* (1849). Both novelist and painter shifted attention from a narrative whole to the specificity of a detailed scene. This shift implied an attack on the conventions of academic art that stressed certain manners in which art was to be composed. Furthermore, these genre conventions specified the interpretive method for extracting poetic meaning from an artwork. Proper interpretation required training and knowledge of both the rules of compositional technique and the allegorical content referenced from Western classical culture.[3] In Flaubert and Courbet we see an attack on these familiar structures of producing and interpreting meaning. The resulting void was filled with a new emphasis on the sensations of the body, or in other words, affect.

This unleashing of the affective body has a political dimension. It provides a new sensible experience for modern reality. Jameson sees in this the creation of an aesthetic identity for the 19th-century bourgeoisie (emerging from the acceleration of capitalism caused in part by the technologies of mechanised industry).[4] This emerging class could no longer find solace in the folk tales of vernacular localities, and actively desired the dismantling of hierarchies enforced by an elite class. Realism emphasises the bodily affects responding to the intensity of sensations in the modern commoditised world.

Abstract and Real

One of the mistakes made many times in criticism regarding 20th-century avant-garde art is to contrast realism with abstraction. This is understandable in the case of the Soviet Union's move from the avant-garde of Constructivism/ Suprematism to Socialist Realism, but even this transition is trickier than Clement Greenberg allows in his essay 'Avant-Garde and Kitsch' (1961).[5] In Greenberg's argument, abstraction is progressive and democratic, while realism is at best kitsch and at worst a tool for repressive political propaganda. This stance perverts the relations between abstraction and realism into a polemical battle. Greenberg shifts the enemy of avant-garde art from being the academic tradition to being the modern mechanical reproduction of commodities.[6] In the process he legitimises kitsch as a modern artistic expression and then proceeds to denigrate it as an art of low taste to appease the masses. In his argument, progressive art is abstract and retrograde art is realist/populist/kitsch. But, if we look closely at both sides of this dichotomy, we find that instead of this either/or choice there are actually multiple moments of abstraction in realism. Specific instances are serial reproduction, decontextualisation, subversion of formal conventions, exposure of materials and techniques, and a questioning of traditional mediums – all aspects of realism that involve the introduction of abstractions.

These elements of abstraction in the aesthetics of realism draw comparison to the theories of 'ostranenie' as put forward by the Russian literary critic Viktor Shklovsky in his 1917 essay translated as either 'Art as Technique' or 'Art as Device'.[7] In his argument, art is that which elongates attention. This process of slowing down and intensifying attention *is* aesthetic experience. 'Defamiliarisation' or estrangement reveals the world to be other than how it is commonly understood to be received. 'And

Most phenomenologically motivated buildings are actually heavily theatrical, employing a multitude of technological effects to create set sequences of phenomenal narratives.

Peter Zumthor, Therme Vals, Graubünden, Switzerland, 1996

The subdued formal expression and emphasised material qualities of the Therme Vals can be considered an expression of phenomenological attention to material and place. Less often commented on is the hidden artifice and technological innovation necessary to produce this fantasy escape into of the primal cave narrative of water, stone and light.

The spectacular formal expression and construction of the abstract skin of the hotel can be considered an expression of otherworldly fantasy affects available through digital technologies. The skin floats, shimmers and glides as a series of shifting colour phenomena. Although its construction is clearly on display, the affect is of an animate mirage.

so, in order to return sensation to our limbs, in order to make us feel objects, to make a stone feel stony, man has been given the tool of art … By "estranging" objects and complicating form, the device of art has a purpose all its own and ought to be extended to the fullest.'[8] The main examples that Shklovsky references are from Tolstoy. These include such devices as the shifting of narrative point of view (from the human to the animal in one instance) and the description of an action solely through qualitative sensations, avoiding all direct naming of the action itself. For these formalist critiques, defamiliarisation operates both at the level of inverted conventions (a conceptual project) and heightened attention (a sensation project).

The Mediation of Sensation

The discourse on sensation has been prominent in contemporary architecture since the early 1990s. These discussions have most often been affiliated with either digital formalism or phenomenological materiality. The fact that a similar concern with sensation unites what are typically seen as diametrically opposed views on architecture should serve to suggest that there may be other issues at stake. The debate between these two sides is not really a question of formal style, but actually a disagreement about mediation. The digital position posits an interest in sensation as derived from the intensification of effects that new media can provoke in the subject. The phenomenological position holds that sensations are intensified by an unmediated experience produced through built architecture.[9] (Digital formalists could be Greg Lynn, Asymptote, Zaha Hadid Architects, UN Studio. Phenomenological materialists could be Juhani Pallasmaa, Steven Holl, Peter Zumthor.) One side places all the emphasis on the technology of mediation, the other on the rejection of all mediation. One side understands the impossibility of having any unmediated experience, the other believes that we can access the real directly through experience. What is absent from both is an acknowledgment of the tensions between reality and representation as put forward through an aesthetics of realism.

The stakes are extremely high. For in the pursuit of formal novelty and ornamental complexity through expertise in digital techniques, much recent work from this segment of architectural design became a kind of fetish cult. The hope was to open new subjectivities through the affective realm stimulated by technology, but what actually happened was a downplaying of the real and a descent into the special effects of fantasy. This result is in many ways similar to the phenomenological materialists. To claim to truly know the spirit of a place, or to have special access to the essence of material, and then believe that the architect can induce these sensations as affective experience in others, is just as fetishistic and just as much a fantasy. Most phenomenologically motivated buildings are actually heavily theatrical, employing a multitude of technological effects to create set sequences of phenomenal narratives.

Both of these movements, the digital and the phenomenological, which were so dominant a generation ago, are under harsh critique today and have faded from popularity in recent years largely due to their inability to directly engage and estrange reality. All of these critiques have their points and merit future consideration, but as with many generational cleansings, what gets thrown out often includes quite a bit of the important gains made by the work under attack.

In the case discussed here, these sacrificial lambs are digital technology and affect theory. It is extremely problematic to begin to take an anti-technological stance regarding digital mediation. The reality of our contemporary world is that it is heavily mediated through computation and digital technologies. To leave a progressive engagement of these aspects out of advanced cultural work is to forfeit these technologies to other fields. Architecture must continue to push forward with digital work while simultaneously understanding that the digital is engaged in a much wider cultural context. It is equally problematic to associate affect only with the digital or phenomenological strains of recent architecture. To avoid questions of affect is to not only ignore a significant aspect of how architecture is received, but also to ignore the political implications that follow from aesthetic provocations.

Lo-Fi/Sci-Fi
An example for clarification can be made by comparing two genres of science-fiction filmmaking. The first is Fantasy Sci-Fi (*Star Wars*, *Avatar*, *The Avengers*, *Transformers*, etc). These films propose aliens, planets, technologies and future worlds. They are largely utopian or dystopian, providing an escape from the everyday world around us. They often draw their stories from grand religious and mythological narratives. These movies retell stories from our collective cultural past, now cast

The reveal also does something else aesthetically – it hyper-realises the abstraction of the modern wall.

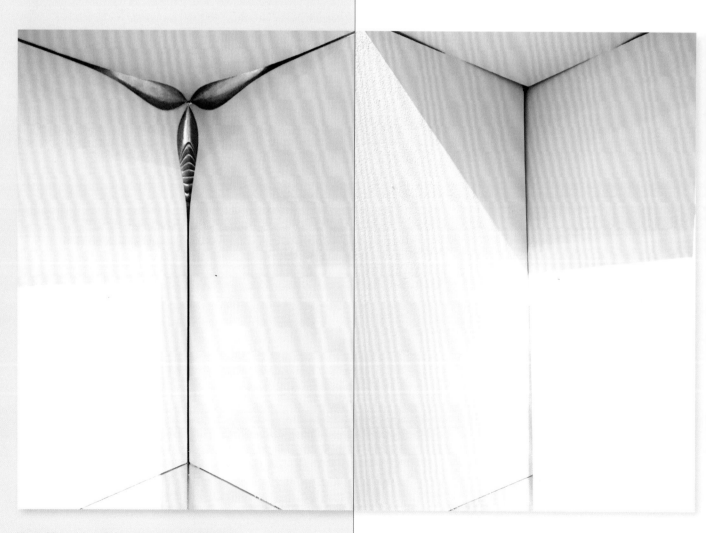

Views of Corners A and B: Corner A reveals the interior corner to be a non-dimensional point. Corner B reveals a slip and flip between which plane appears in front and which appears behind.

in the special effects of fantasy aesthetics. The second genre is called Lo-Fi/Sci-Fi (*Europa Report*, *Moon*, *Anti-Viral*, *Primer*, *Her*, etc). These films typically take place in the very near future, if not actually in a world that feels uncannily similar to our own. They establish their aesthetics through fragments of highly descriptive scenes as opposed to a narrative whole. It is once this filmic world is believed as operating in the everyday that the films begin to insert elements that destabilise this reality. These changes, or tensions, primarily take a contemporary problem and accelerate it into the near future.

It should also be clear that Lo-Fi/Sci-Fi films, even with smaller budgets, produce stranger affects. In fact it is very hard to give them a clean genre: they sometimes create sensations of dread, but not horror; they are often funny, but not because they have jokes; there are moments of intense drama, but rarely through character destruction and redemption. These films more often than not make the viewer uncomfortable. They primarily produce affective states that are difficult to categorise or name, which is of course the exact connection that Jameson makes between realism and affect in the 19th century. When these films are at their best, they provide a speculative reality where through aesthetics, political questions begin to emerge. The viewer is asked to think differently about the reality surrounding them as opposed to escaping into the fantasy of a future world.

Views of Corners C and D: Corner C reveals the interior corner to project back into the depth of the wall. Corner D reveals the corner as a bar that passes vertically through the ceiling.

View of Corner A construction. The entire detail is built from off-the-shelf materials using common construction methods: wood studs and joists, Simpson joist hangers, half-inch gypsum board and exposed warehouse fixtures. The only exceptions are the reveals, which are custom 3D prints.

View of Corner B construction. The most successful corner. At first glance it is hard to notice what is happening; it appears that the wall is somehow wrong. The reveal disappears to estrange the wall itself.

View of Corner C construction. This corner has two aspects. At the ceiling the reveal pulls back into the space of the wall cavity, well beyond the amount of space that could actually exist. Towards the bottom, the reveal squeezes out of the wall to become a convex solid in front.

View of Corner D construction. This is the most formally expressive detail in that there are both gold reveals that recede and 3D-printed pieces painted white that cusp up in front of the wall surface. The push and pull becomes more of an ornamental motif rippling the corner intersections.

The Everyday Reveal

The arguments put forward in this essay were explored recently in Young & Ayata's Wall Reveal (2016), a full-scale construction detail exhibited at the 'Close-Up' group exhibition at the SCI-Arc Gallery, Los Angeles, in the spring of 2016. The constructed object investigates the Fry Reglet gypsum board reveal. The reveal is one of the most common details operating in the background of contemporary architecture. It is barely visible, just a shadow. It has become the default detail to resolve the joint between walls, floors, ceilings and apertures. It is pragmatic when providing a hard edge to finish the gypsum board and 'modern' in its removal of decorative baseboards, mouldings and trim pieces that conceal construction in traditional architecture. But the reveal also does something else aesthetically – it hyper-realises the abstraction of the modern wall. The shadow line of the reveal produces walls that appear to float without any evidence of thickness or assembly; walls become immaterial planes.

It is into these typical reveal details that Young & Ayata has jacked four different interventions. These intrusions disturb the assumed background of the modern abstract wall. With minimal modifications only on the reveals, it is no longer clear where a corner is, how thick a wall is, or what plane is in front of the other.

The construction also opens an estrangement of scale relations. From afar the piece appears as a fragment of typical construction. Up close, inside the gypsum board spaces, the appearance is of a finished interior. It is at the middle distance between these two extremes that an unstable relation to scale becomes aesthetically triggered. The gap between the two scales is hard to maintain simultaneously, making certain elements take on the abstract qualities of a scale model while other elements flip towards appearing too large, over-scaled. All this occurs even though every part of the construction is full-scale reality.

This project advances a connection between affect and realism in contemporary digital architecture. Importantly, the digitally designed and fabricated reveals are not the foreground of attention. They are inserted into the background of a completely typical construction detail. It is here that they attempt to unsettle the background of what is commonly assumed to constitute the realism of construction. When they are at their most successful, it is not the detail that draws attention to it as a special effect, but instead an affective sensation is triggered that there is something strange in the entire situation. The aesthetic effect is to defamiliarise the wall itself. The common everyday gypsum board wall becomes revealed as the abstract decoration that it actually is.

These often-overlooked affects of small details are instances where architecture produces the aesthetic background of reality. As Walter Benjamin famously suggests: 'Architecture has always offered the prototype of an artwork that is received in a state of distraction and through the collective.'[9] A distinction that should not be read as a lessening of its importance. By being perceived habitually, architecture establishes what most people assume to be 'the real'. Understood in this manner, the questions of defamiliarisation, and the opening of new affective realms through the aesthetics of realism, are a crucial architectural concern. This is where architecture can focus an acceleration of its engagement with technology. Not as fantasy in the production of novelty, but through the ways that aesthetics can put into tension assumptions regarding reality. Architecture can make the background glitch, stutter, bend, and through these errors or gaps provide opportunities for doubt, intensifications of attention and an affective realm of sensation. ⊿

The entire catalogue of custom reveals used in the four corner details. It is interesting to compare these to the catalogue of typical details from the Fry Reglet metals company. Both sets are fairly strange when extracted from their installed context. It is once they have entered into construction that the questions of an estranged realism begin to emerge.

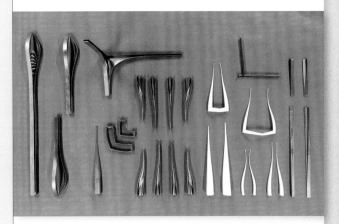

The aesthetic defamiliarises the wall itself, revealed now as the abstract decoration that it actually is.

Notes
1. Fredric Jameson, *The Antinomies of Realism*, Verso (New York), 2013, pp 10–11.
2. *Ibid*, p 29.
3. Jacques Rancière, *The Politics of Aesthetics*, Continuum (New York), 2004, pp 21–2.
4. Fredric Jameson, *op cit*, p 32.
5. Clement Greenberg, 'Avant-Garde and Kitsch', *Art and Culture*, Beacon Press (Boston, MA), 1961, pp 18–19.
6. Boris Groys, *In the Flow*, Verso (New York), 2016, p 107.
7. Viktor Shklovsky, 'Art as Device' [1917], *Theory of Prose*, Dalkey Archive Press (London), 1991.
8. *Ibid*, p 6.
9. Walter Benjamin, 'The Work of Art in the Age of its Technological Reproducibility: Second Version', *The Work of Art in the Age of its Technological Reproducibility, and Other Writings on Media*, Harvard University Press (Cambridge, MA), 2008, p 40.

François Roche with Camille Lacadée

Parrhesia-stases (The Preamble)

Operating between the obscene and methods of estrangement and displacement, parrhesia-stases interrogates the agendas of aesthetics present in repulsiveness, condemnation and punishment. **François Roche and Camille Lacadée** here present a body of work by their Bangkok-based practice New-Territories/M4, which speculates on the ramifications of architecture as a paradigm of disobedience. Deeply rooted in Michel Foucault's proposal for a re-evaluation of an ethico-political approach, the work investigates an alternative architectural position that utilises strategies of transfiguration to provoke pathological behaviours.

w-Territories/M4 and the
Alfred Taubman College
Architecture and Urban
sign, mythomaniaS –
ncrete[I]Land, University
Michigan, Ann Arbor,
chigan, 2015

ove: Seismographic extrusion by
bot, a real-time sensor interface
edback with reading-book analogue
outs and matter of mud and human
eces extracted from the slum, all
aking out in an ecosophical loop of
atter, of digestive substances.

posite: View below the freeway, and
er the swamp – dirty but human.
e site has a population of 2 tonnes
shit components, each of them
ique, metabolised and petrified by
ices as a reminder of the content –
s a library.

Going beyond what has already happened, facing a posthumous text, collateral effect or artefact of the 'architecture of moods' stuttered in a previous 𝐷,[1] we can now unfold the parrhesia-stases epilogue.

It is happening backstage, 'offstage',[2] behind the wall, the curtain. And someone on the wall is telling you about it. What happens there, behind the wall, is horrid, disgusting, repulsive, offensive, obscene – however, it will be the one who tells the story, who reports it, who will be accused of obscenity. And that is where obscenity is; its difference from intimacy is that it belongs to everyone. It is because you 'see' it that it is obscenity, because you recognise it – and indeed we always shoot the messenger.

The obscene is looking at you.

The scene of course is off-scene, and if it stayed off-scene it would not be considered off-scene (obscene). It is because of this transcript that the obscene is reached. However, if you can 'see it', it is because you know it, you know that place, you have been there, but you do not want anyone to know about that, although it is clear that they all know as well.

Obscenity is a trigger for the imagination (like what happens off-screen in a film, often more powerful than what we are given to witness) and it turns the 'victim' guilty.

It is on this wall, on this frontier, that freedom of speech is at stake; it collapses on the other side, but it remains here ambiguous. Looking now at how the laws evolved regarding this matter, we understand the society we now live in much better. For if these matters begin with self-censorship, they are then controlled and implemented by governments through the apparatuses of law, quite quietly, at first imprecisely, clumsily, almost innocently, as an administered legal management of self-censorship. Nowadays reaching deplorable proportions with the self-policing of social networks, and latest offspring of the cultural hegemony.[3]

*Can the obscene exist without
its implied condemnation
and subsequent punishment?*

New-Territories/M4,
mythomaniaS -Ex-timity,
2016

right: Secretion of bioplastic with
perturbations and stochastic positioning,
in real time, where the trajectory of the
nozzle reacts to the robot's secreting
noises and running sounds transformed
into feedback schizoid data.

opposite: Encrustation of the main
character, shiny and gloomy, sweaty and
smelly. In extimacy she enters herself and
confronts her nudity, her desire to show it
off, innocent(?) of boundaries and morals.
To the limits of eroticism, extasis, enstasis
versus intimacy.

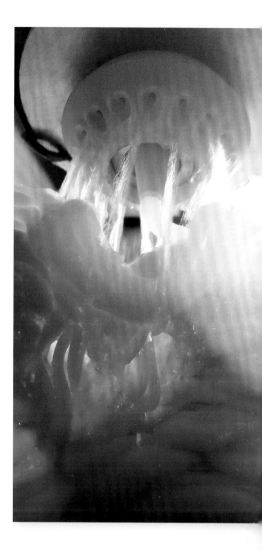

Obscene turned inside out into showing off its own guts.

But what is the object of repulsion here? It is not the totem, but the act,
the weakness of the act, the surrendering to it that is condemned. Can
the obscene exist without its implied condemnation and subsequent
punishment?

The laws only reveal their own weaknesses towards it. Their difficulty in
framing what is to be condemned as obscene is almost touching, refusing to
name what is nothing else than the bourgeois moral code, the society Freud
studied from within.

And transgression only eats its very definition. We can have exceptional
authors who flirt with these boundaries, but don't we know that exception
confirms the rule. We should rather think of a society that would deal
differently with objects and aesthetics of repression, a society that
probably then would not be relying solely upon consumerism of goods
and information, or as we see it today, of nothing – for to consume is a
satisfying act in itself, and does not need in fact a product to be consumed –
as its main structural social binder in a strategy of political fiction as defined
by Louis Althusser.[4]

Let us go together behind the wall for a little while, and see what is there –
secret, hidden, concealed, kept behind, in the crypt.

New-Territories/M4, mythomaniaS - Euthanasia,
St Moritz, Switzerland, 2015

top: Aluminium mould for vacuum thermoforming. The rippling
surfaces are created by temperature-sensor variations.

centre: Accumulation of human bas-relief (5 metres/16 feet high)
as the last shelter. The project addresses the issue of teenage
suicide in the Swiss Alps during the winter months where
hypothermia becomes a method of euthanasia.

bottom: The solitude of the suicide, at 2,000 metres (6,560 feet)
high, in full winter, –25˚C, in a protest against the Swiss political
policy of hypothermia versus euthanasia.

tes
See François Roche, 'Next-Door Instructions', AD The
w Pastoralism: Landscape Into Architecture, May/June
) 3), 2013, pp 126–33. An architecture 'des humeurs'
09–11) is based on the potential that contemporary
ences offer to reread human corporalities via their
ysiology and chemical balance. This assumption
empts to make palpable and graspable, through
hnologies, the emotional transactions of the 'body
mal', the body headless, the chemistry of the body,
that these psycho-physio technologies inform us of
adaptation, sympathy and empathy, confronted with
articular situation, with the sensitive perception of
environment. See www.new-territories.com/blog/
hitecturedeshumeurs/.
Derived from the Latin *'obscaena'* (offstage), a cognate
the Ancient Greek root *'skene'*. In classical drama,
me potentially offensive content, such as murder or
<, was depicted offstage in an *obscaena* situation.
Cultural hegemony' is a term developed by Antonio
amsci, activist, theorist and founder of the Communist
ty of Italy. It describes the domination of a culturally
erse society by the ruling class, who manipulate
culture of that society – the beliefs, explanations,
rceptions, values and mores – so that their ruling-class
rldview becomes the worldview that is imposed and
cepted as the cultural norm, as the universally valid
minant ideology that justifies the social, political and
onomic status quo as natural, inevitable, perpetual
d beneficial for everyone, rather than as artificial social
nstructs that benefit only the ruling class.
Althusser argues that even the parliamentary structures
the state, constituted by the delegation of its citizens
d their will, their free-will, is an 'ideological state
paratus' involving the 'fiction, corresponding to a
ertain" reality, that the component parts of the system,
well as the principle of its functioning, are based on
ideology of the "freedom" and "equality" of the
lividual voters and the "free choice" of the people's
presentatives by the individuals that "make up" the
ople.' See Louis Althusser, *On the Reproduction of
pitalism*, Verso (London and New York), 2014, pp 222–3.
Parrhesia, is a figure of fearless speech: 'to speak
ndidly or to ask forgiveness for so speaking'. See
chel Foucault, 'Discourse and Truth', six lectures at the
iversity of California Berkeley, October to November
'3: www.openculture.com/2014/10/michel-foucaults-
al-uc-berkeley-lectures-discourse-and-truth-1983.
nl; and Foucault, *The Government of Self and Others:
ctures at the Collège de France 1982–1983*, Palgrave
cmillan (Basingstoke), 2011, which includes 'The
urage of Truth', the last series of lectures before his
ath in 1984.
Concrete[I]Land: New-Territories/
ndMachineMakingMyth – François Roche with Camille
cadée, Daniela Mitterberger and Vong Wongkillalerd;
Alfred Taubman College – Po-Jen Huang, Te-Shiou
en, Jakkrit Jannakhon, Linnea Cook, Salam Rida, Min
ang, Weiqi Zhang, Stefan Klecheski, Beth Carliner,
er Sepassi, Tracey Weisman and John Yoon. Ex-timity:
w-Territories/MindMachineMakingMyth – François
che with Camille Lacadée, Stephan Henrich, Daniela
terberger, Vong Wongkillalerd, Benjamin Ennemoser
d Joey Jacobson, with the support of Graham
undation, CNC France.

Beyond this obscene and psychotic cavern, New-Territories/M4's mythomaniaS project (2011–16) refers to the last research of Michel Foucault, mainly about the notion of 'parrhesia'[5] – a strategy of discourse, attitude and form that re-evaluates the ethico-political approach facing social conformism. Foucault developed this concept through the transfiguration of Charles Baudelaire, through the posture of alteration by Cynic philosophical decay, with the figure among others of Diogenes, and through the method of 'estrangement' as a displacement of values by Allen Ginsberg. The Diogenes agenda, as an aesthetic of the being, has to be understood, according to Foucault, as an intentional enterprise of falsification of 'the habit and currency'. Organised around the celebration of the human-beast or the beast-human, the critical and performative borderline is used as a weapon to corrupt the repetition of conventional routines and discourses to operate, ultimately, a strategy of transformation, of transfiguration of what is politic, of what we should consider as politic. It is about to make visible the singular dimension, through the contingencies of the arbitrary constraints, inside of what is considered as universal, necessary and obligatory.

Architecture is used in our systemicism, as a 'paradigm of disobedience', to paraphrase Henry Thoreau or Étienne de La Boetie – as an experiment of what should not have been revealed, able to help us to get back our voice, our scream, through what Foucault defines as the 'truth', which cannot emerge in another way than through an alterity, extreme and radical.[6] AD

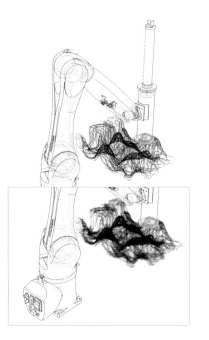

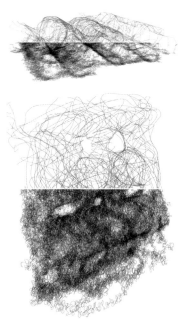

w-Territories/M4, mythomaniaS - Robotic
al-time sensor interfaces, 2011-16

sitions of the nozzle, of trajectories, of robot as
nditional, between 'the point where the machine was'
d 'the point where the machine should be', as a vector
translation in an iterative research on unreachable
nts. The agents, as noise/sound of the machine, corrupt
programmed predictable workflow and modify the
rication path in real time as a stuttering feedback from
intrinsic protocol of doing, increasing the intricate
anders of the tool in an ever permanent inaccuracy of
sitioning, introducing nonlinear processes as a way to
ger pathologised technologies.

Text © 2016 John Wiley & Sons Ltd.
Images © New-Territories/M4

Affects of Intricate Mass

The Strange Characteristics of the RMIT Mace and NGV Pavilion

The use of iterative multi-agent algorithms to produce an accretion of intricate mass, rather than predefined form, is a key focus of current research at **Roland Snooks**'s Melbourne studio. Here the architect and senior lecturer presents two projects, on very different scales, which his practice has developed using this 'behavioural formation' process, in collaboration with RMIT University. Defined by complex fibrous assemblages rather than surface or volume, they offer weird and wonderful atmospheric affects.

Studio Roland Snooks,
NGV Pavilion,
National Gallery of Victoria,
Melbourne,
2016

A dense volume of fibres that unravels and frays at its edges defines the intricate mass of the pavilion.

Mass defined by the accretion of fibrous elements creates an alternative reading of form from that of surface, volume or lattice, one that is rich with intricate detail and strange characteristics. The atmospheric affects, or mood, of intricate mass are central to the design of two recent projects carried out at Studio Roland Snooks and RMIT University in Melbourne. The RMIT Mace, designed in collaboration with Scott Mayson, was commissioned for the university's ceremonial events. A turbulent, unfurling mass, it reinterprets the intricate and ornamental characteristics of its historical counterparts. The deep labyrinths of fibrous titanium that characterise the form compress into swirling surfaces at the object's extremities. In contrast, the NGV Pavilion, a proposal for the National Gallery of Victoria's summer Architecture Commission, is defined by boulder-like volumes that delaminate or flake into surfaces. The forms of both projects unravel at their edges, creating a balance between mass and filigree.

The work of Studio Roland Snooks explores the strange specificity of objects that emerges from behavioural processes of formation. A primary concern is the affectual capacities of the objects, however their characteristics are intrinsically tied to the nature and behaviour of the computational and material processes through which they are designed and fabricated. The RMIT Mace and NGV Pavilion projects therefore defy contemporary considerations of objects as autonomous to their formation. Their characteristics and atmospheric affects resist being drawn or explicitly modelled. Instead, their intensity, resolution and complex order are emergent properties of the volatile self-organising interaction of populations of fibrous bodies.

Roland Snooks
and Scott Mayson,
RMIT Mace,
d—lab,
RMIT University,
Melbourne,
2015

The character of the mace shifts
from a compressed mass to a
volatile unfurling of topologically
complex porous surfaces.

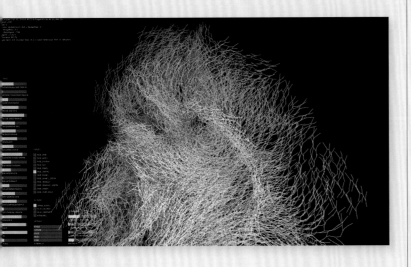

The form is generated through the interaction design and fabrication behaviours encoded within a multi-agent algorithm.

Below: Deep, fibrous labyrinths rather than surface or volume defines the turbulent form.

Right: The complex geometry of the mace is fabricated through a selective laser melting process that prints the fibrous elements at a thickness of 0.3 millimetres.

This approach is part of the practice's ongoing 'behavioural formation' design research agenda, which focuses on designing through the behaviour of multi-agent algorithms. The strategy employed in both the RMIT Mace and NGV Pavilion encodes the formal, ornamental, structural and fabrication behaviours within the body of the agent. Rather than the increasingly common and somewhat banal approach to multi-agent design that simply traces the path of the agent, this strategy self-organises the geometry and negotiates diverse design intentions.

The formal characteristics of the projects are dependent upon the interaction of the algorithmic generation of mass and directly modelled volumes. This interaction tempers their turbulent generative topologies, compressing the fibrous mass to the surface of the volume, which forms the handle of the mace and the boulder-like objects of the pavilion. This flattening amplifies the patterns or ornamental qualities of the objects through the local suppression of spatial complexity. The volumes are deliberately open-ended to enable a balance between the explicit and the generative, creating readings of surface, mass, solidity and intricate spatial organisations.

The volumes are deliberately open-ended to enable a balance between the explicit and the generative, creating readings of surface, mass, solidity and intricate spatial organisations.

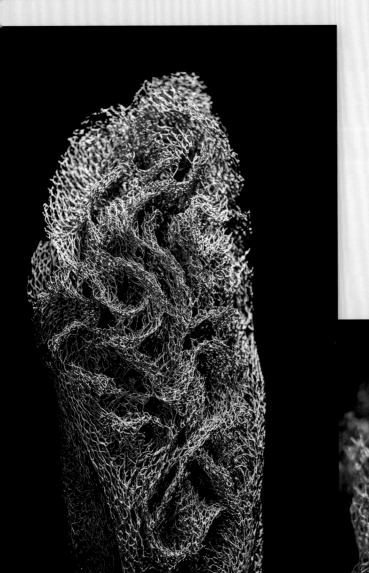

Studio Roland Snooks,
NGV Pavilion,
National Gallery
of Victoria,
Melbourne,
2016

The form of the pavilion is defined by
the interaction and feedback between
volatile algorithmic processes and
explicitly modelled forms.

This volatility focuses design intention on character rather than on form.

above: An intricate network of
concrete structural members is cast
within the veins of the polymer skin.

Constructing these intricate geometries and their nuanced relationship between surface and lattice requires direct deposition fabrication technologies. The mace leverages titanium selective laser melting techniques capable of printing each fibre of the mass at a width of 0.3 millimetres. The fabrication of the pavilion, however, operates at a vastly different scale – robotically printed with a 5-millimetre polymer skin to produce a permanent formwork within which the concrete structural members are cast. The large populations of elements that comprise each mass prohibit the post-rationalisation of their geometry to fulfil fabrication requirements. They must therefore be encoded within the agent model to establish a methodology in which the wild generative processes of the objects are conditioned by the constraints of fabrication.

The characteristics of intricate mass of the RMIT Mace and NGV Pavilion thus arise from the volatile behaviour of their agents, their geometry, interaction with explicitly modelled volumes and the processes of fabrication. This volatility focuses design intention on character rather than on form. Form, gesture and silhouette are external to the ontology of the algorithms that generate these intricate masses, while sensitivity to initial conditions within the algorithmic process resists design intention at this macro scale. Instead, the nature of the topology, the thickness of the swirling mass and its compression to manifold surfaces are emergent outcomes of iteratively refined design intentions encoded within the behaviour of the algorithms. This represents a shift from designing form to designing the accretion of mass imbued with atmospheric spatial affects from which the strange characteristics of the objects emerge. ⚙

elow: The surface of the polymer rototype is fabricated through a botic extrusion technique.

Mario Carpo

Excessive

From Digital Streamlining to
Computational Complexity

Alisa Andrasek
and Jose Sanchez/
Bloom Games, Bloom,
Victoria Park,
London, 2012

Visual opulence versus
the elegant simplification
of science: modern maths
aimed at simple scripts and
begot streamlined shapes;
postmodern computation
needs neither.

Resolution

s the term 'ornament' set to become redundant in
rchitecture? With the sinuous lines produced by CNC
nilling machines giving way to the ever more weirdly
igural products of algorithmically controlled 3D printing,
lecoration is increasingly an integral part of form,
ather than supplementary to it. **Mario Carpo** – Reyner
3anham Professor of Architectural Theory and History
t the Bartlett School of Architecture, University College
London – investigates this voxellisation, and how it
Irives architecture beyond human comprehension.

Foreign Office
Architects (FOA),
Yokohama International
Port Terminal,
Yokohama, Japan, 2002

One of the first and seminal
examples of NURBS-inspired
architecture. Regardless of
the software that was actually
employed for this project,
the continuity of form, lines,
surfaces and flow is at the core
of its programme.

Digitally intelligent architecture no longer looks the way it did. The style that marked the first digital turn in the 1990s was famously sinuous and streamlined. What we see today in the digital labs of most schools looks messy, disjointed, fuzzy, filamentous or at times excessively and weirdly figural. Back in the 1990s, the first style of the spline was all about smooth continuity and elegant simplicity; today, 3D-printed voxels and extruded filaments are shown as they come and as they are – that is, as complex and discrete, sometimes unintelligible aggregations of matter.

Old Maths

As I have argued elsewhere,[1] one of the reasons behind this drastic change of mood, which is in fact a change in our culture at large, and in the technologies we use, is that in the beginning we used computers to implement an older science – that of Galileo and Newton, of Descartes and Leibniz. Splines have been handcrafted since the beginning of time, but the maths of the spline is very old, too: calculus (which we use to calculate smoothness) is a late baroque invention; Bézier's and De Casteljau's methods for the mathematical notation of free form lines and surfaces (eventually known as NURBS) were developed between 1958 and 1964 – and without the use of any computer, other than the engineer's slide rule.

Today, to the contrary, digitally intelligent designers more and more often adopt problem-solving algorithms that are specific to computational tools, even when they are incompatible with our own mental processes, or they transcend the limits of modern science as we knew it. Strange as it may seem, computers are at long last developing their own kind of science – and, not surprisingly, some of us like that and some do not.

Philippe Morel/EZCT Architecture
& Design Research, T1-M 860
Computational Chair, 2004

An early and seminal example of computationally
driven structural optimisation resulting in the
display of a voxellated aggregate.

The messy point clouds, filament bundles and volumetric units of design and calculation that result from these processes are now increasingly shown in all of their apparent messiness, and one of the earliest styles resulting from this mode of composition has often been called voxellisation, or voxellation. The Computational Chair Studies by Philippe Morel of EZCT Architecture & Design Research in 2004 were among the earliest demonstrations of this approach, and the ArchiLab 2013 exhibition at the FRAC Centre in Orléans, France, reveals this formal landscape at a glance (see for example the works of Alisa Andrasek and Jose Sanchez or by Matias del Campo and Sandra Manninger). Subdivisions-based programs originally used to simulate continuous curves and surfaces, are now often tweaked to achieve the opposite effect, and segments or patches are left large enough for the surface to look rough or angular. Discreteness is also at the basis of the method of finite elements, now embedded in most software for structural design, which represents in many ways an early example of 'agnostic' science,[2] where the prediction of structural behaviour is separated from causal interpretation.

Other examples could follow, but the spirit of the game is the same: in all such instances, designers use the power of today's computation to notate reality as it appears at any chosen scale, without converting it into simplified and scalable mathematical formulas or laws. The inherent discreteness of nature (which, after all, is not made of dimensionless Euclidean points nor of continuous mathematical lines, but of distinct chunks of matter, all the way down to molecules, atoms and electrons) is then captured and kept as it comes, ideally, or in practice as close to its material structure as needed, with all of the apparent randomness and irregularity that will inevitably show at each scale of resolution. The manufacturing tool that best interpreted the spirit of continuity of the age of spline-making was the CNC milling machine, a legacy subtractive fabrication technology which, using computer-controlled drills, could – at its best – simulate the sweeping, smooth and continuous gestures of the hand of a skilled craftsman – a sculptor, but also a baker or a wax modeller.

SPAN (Matias del Campo and Sandra Manninger), Barcelona Recursion, 2010

From data-starved to data-opulent: computation abandons simplification and streamlining to embrace complexity and engage with the 'excessive' resolution of nature as it is.

Greg Lynn, Installation at 'Expanding the Gap' exhibition, Cologne Furniture Fair, Rendel & Spitz Gallery, Cologne, 2002

The CNC toolpath becomes the outward and visible form of the inner workings of mathematical spline modelling.

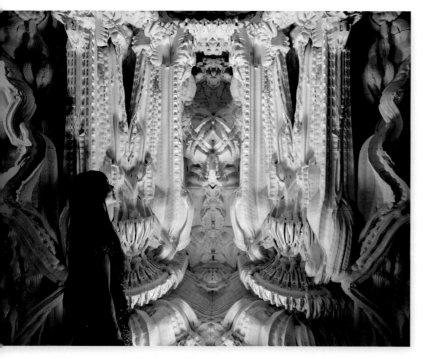

Michael Hansmeyer with Benjamin Dillenburger, *Grotto Prototype*, ArchiLab 2013, *Naturaliser l'architecture – Naturalizing Architecture*, FRAC Centre, Orléans, France

left: The new technical logic of 3D printing upends the traditional notions of decoration and ornament, and belies the notational legacy of Western architectural design. If these intricate surfaces do not follow any mathematical rule, who could notate all 30 billion of them one by one? In fact, if one looks at the computational nuts and bolts of the project, that is not how the grotto was designed and made.

Adolf Loos, *Ornament and Crime*, lecture poster, 21 February 1913

right: Loos's lecture, first given in Vienna in January 1910, was a staple of Modernist theories against wasteful ornament – even though Loos himself was far from being a puritan censor of conspicuous consumption.

Not surprisingly, the CNC milling machine was the iconic tool of the 1990s, and there was a time when every school of architecture in the world had or wanted one. Today the 3D printer has taken its place: an additive fabrication technology, where each voxel must be individually designed, calculated and made. At the time of writing, 3D printing is as influential for a new generation of digital designers as 3D milling was 15 years ago. This is ostensibly due to a number of developments in manufacturing technologies, but the two processes are also based on contrary, indeed incompatible, informational logics.

A New Computational Logic

CNC milling may be as data-rich as one wants it to be, or as much as the machine allows, but in the absence of signal (in the case of zero-data input) digital subtractive technologies will still work – and deliver a plain, solid chunk of matter: in most cases, releasing the original surface in its pristine material state, unmarked and without any denting, milling or amputation. This means that digital milling, in case of need, may do with few data, or even with no data – and indeed designers using digital subtractive technologies apply data to inform matter only as and where needed. Each 3D-printed voxel, to the contrary, needs a certain amount of data and of machine time: in the absence of signal (ie, in the case of zero data input) additive fabrication delivers nothing at all.

Furthermore, as each voxel is individually printed, and 3D printing does not involve any reusable cast, mould, stamp or die, there is no need, and no incentive, to make any voxel-generated volume identical to any other, regardless of scale or size. Mechanical printing technologies are matrix based, and any matrix, once made, must be used as many times as possible to amortise its cost. But standardisation does not deliver any economy of scale in a digital design and fabrication workflow: just as 20 years ago we learned that we could laser print 100 different pages, or 100 identical copies of the same page, at the same unit cost, today we know we can 3D print any given volume of a given material at the same volumetric cost, based on the number of voxels that compose it (ie, on resolution), not on geometry or configuration (that is, regardless of where each printed voxel will be relative to all others in the same volume). An economist would say that the marginal production cost of a voxel is always the same, no matter how many we print – and irrespective of how they will be assembled. Thus 3D printing brings the logic of digital mass-customisation from the macro scale of product design to the micro scale of the production of physical matter, and at previously unimaginable levels of complexity and granularity: recent 3D printers can create objects with variable densities and in multiple materials.

These simple technical truisms have remarkable consequences. Let us consider a seminal example of monumental 3D printing, the now famous digital Grotto commissioned to Michael Hansmeyer and Benjamin Dillenburger by the Frac Centre and shown there as part of the Archilab exhibition in the summer of 2013. In spite of and against all appearances, the Grotto was not carved from a block (in the subtractive way); it was printed from dust, that is, almost from nothing, in the additive way. As a result, the Grotto we see, including all of its intricate details, was faster and cheaper to make than a plain full block of that size (if printed at the same resolution), simply because all the void inside the Grotto was not printed. If we had wanted the plain full block, we should have kept printing – and we would have kept spending. Likewise, any onlooker familiar with the traditional (manual or mechanical, or even early digital) ways of making, may instinctively assume that the astoundingly intricate detailing of Hansmeyer's and Dillenburger's Grotto must have cost even more labour and money – that is, labour and money that would have been saved had this detailing not been added on. Not so: as all 260 million surfaces in this 30-billion voxel space had to be individually 3D printed, the technical cost of delivering the same number of voxels in regular rows, so as to create plain, flat and regular surfaces, would have been exactly the same.

his is rather a counterintuitive result, as we tend to think that ecoration, or ornament, are expensive, and the more decoration e want, the more we have to pay for it. But in the case of lansmeyer's and Dillenburger's Grotto, the details and ornament e see inside the Grotto, oddly, made it cheaper. This is of course nly true in theory, if we disregard the time and cost of designing ach voxel one by one – an operation that appears to have taken n inordinate amount of time, and which is in fact entirely ependent upon some drastic computational shortcuts (which lansmeyer and Dillenburger have documented in a number of echnical papers).[3] All the same, the difference in technical and heoretical terms between the old and the new way of making striking, indeed revolutionary. Since the beginning of modern mes, indeed since Leon Battista Alberti, Western architectural heory has developed a systematic theory of ornament as upplement: something that is added on top of an object, or of building, and which can be taken away if necessary.[4] But for his very reason, puritans, Taylorists and Modernists of all sorts ave always blamed ornament as waste, superfluity and, in Adolf oos's famous slogan, a crime – labour and capital thrown out of he window, money that should have been better spent in some ther way.

now appears that the technical and cultural premises of all his are simply not true anymore. In the age of Big Data and D printing, decoration is no longer an addition; ornament is o longer a supplemental expense; hence the very same terms f decoration and ornament, predicated as they are on the raditional Western notion of ornament as supplement and uperfluity, do not apply, and perhaps we should simply discard nese terms, together with the meanings they still convey.[5] his opens a Pandora's box of theoretical issues, which in turn ndermine some core aesthetic and architectural principles of oth the Classical and Modernist traditions.

The End of Ornament

Similar arguments have also been recently invoked to construe a theory of today's digital style as one of figural realism, excessive realism or digital hyperrealism. In an interesting and quirky book just published, polymath designer and theoretician Michael Young relates the richness in detail and figural sumptuosity that are increasingly transparent in some of the work of today's digital avant-garde to the 'weird realism' that Graham Harman famously attributes to horror fiction writer HP Lovecraft (a cyberpunk and speculative realism cult writer, as well as the subject of the first published essay by acclaimed misanthropic writer Michel Houellebecq).[6] Assuredly, excessive resolution is a diacritical stylistic trait of the second digital style, and it has reasons to appear 'weird'. Excessive resolution is the outward and visible sign of an inward and invisible excess of data: a reminder of a technical logic we may master and unleash, but that we can neither replicate, emulate, nor even simply comprehend with our mind. This may be one reason why the emergence of some inchoate form of artificial intelligence in technology and in the arts already warrants a more than robust amount of natural discomfort: the feeling of 'alienation', which originally, in the works of a great critique of the Industrial Revolution, now often forgotten, meant the industrial separation of the hands of the makers from the tools of production[7] may just as well be applied today to the ongoing post-industrial separation of the minds of the thinkers from the tools of computation. ⌂

PAN (Matias del ampo and Sandra anninger), Ore ashion Stores, hanghai, 2015

D-printed concrete an be as variable nd adaptive as the and-made artisanal pe. Modern industry eeded standard shapes nd form to be able to otate, calculate and bricate predictable uilding materials; none these limitations ply today in a digital esign and production orkflow.

Notes
1. This article derives in part from chapters 2.8 to 2.9 in Mario Carpo, *The Second Digital Turn*, to be published by the MIT Press in 2017. See also Mario Carpo, 'Breaking the Curve: Big Data and Digital Design', *Artforum*, 52 (6), 2014, pp 168–73.
2. See Domenico Napoletani, Marco Panza and Daniele C Struppa, 'Agnostic Science: Towards a Philosophy of Data Analysis', *Foundations of Science*, 16 (1), 2011, pp 1–20.
3. See Benjamin Dillenburger and Michael Hansmeyer, 'The Resolution of Architecture in the Digital Age', in Jianlong Zhang and Chengyu Sun (eds), *Global Design and Local Materialization: 15th International Conference, CAAD Futures 2013, Shanghai, China, July 3–5, 2013 – Proceedings*, Springer Verlag (Berlin and Heidelberg), 2013, pp 347–57; and 'Mesh Grammars: Procedural Articulation of Form', in Rudi Stouffs, Patrick Janssen, Stanislav Roudavski and Bige Tunçer (eds), *Open Systems: Proceedings of the 18th International Conference on Computer-Aided Architectural Design Research in Asia*, CAADRIA (Hong Kong), 2013, pp 821–29.
4. Leon Battista Alberti, *De Re Aedificatoria*, ed and trans Giovanni Orlandi, Il Polifilo (Milan), 1966, pp 447–49; *On the Art of Building in Ten Books*, trans Joseph Rykwert, Neil Leach and Robert Tavernor, MIT Press (Cambridge, MA), 1988, p 156.
5. Several publications bear witness to a recent surge of interest in the theory of ornament, suggesting a widespread awareness of the extent to which digital tools have altered the Western idea of it, both in the classical and in the Modernist traditions. See, for example, Farshid Moussavi and Michael Kubo, *The Function of Ornament*, Actar (Barcelona), 2006; Alina Payne, *From Ornament to Object: Genealogies of Architectural Modernism*, Yale University Press (New Haven, CT and London), 2012; and Antoine Picon, *Ornament: The Politics of Architecture and Subjectivity*, John Wiley & Sons (Chichester), 2013.
6. Young & Ayata/Michael Young, *The Estranged Object*, The Treatise Project c/o The Graham Foundation (Chicago, IL), 2015, pp 45–51; Graham Harman, *Weird Realism: Lovecraft and Philosophy*, Zero Books (Winchester), 2012; Michel Houellebecq, *HP Lovecraft: contre le monde, contre la vie*, Éditions du Rocher (Monaco), 1991.
7. Karl Marx's theory of alienation (estrangement, *Entfremdung* in Marx's original) is outlined in the *Economic and Philosophic Manuscripts of 1844*: see in particular the First Manuscript, chapters XXIII–XXIV.

Something Else, Something Raw

From ProtoHouse to Blokhut: The Aesthetics of Computational Assemblage

London-based architect **Gilles Retsin** is seeking out a new spatial experience. Enough of refined and carefully articulated surfaces and volumes. As demonstrated by these projects from his own practice and from the Softkill Design team – of which he is also a member – new digital techniques make it possible to devise environments that are infused with raw atmosphere. Here, the boundaries between interior and exterior, or between classic elements such as wall, floor and ceiling, are blurred to the point of nonexistence.

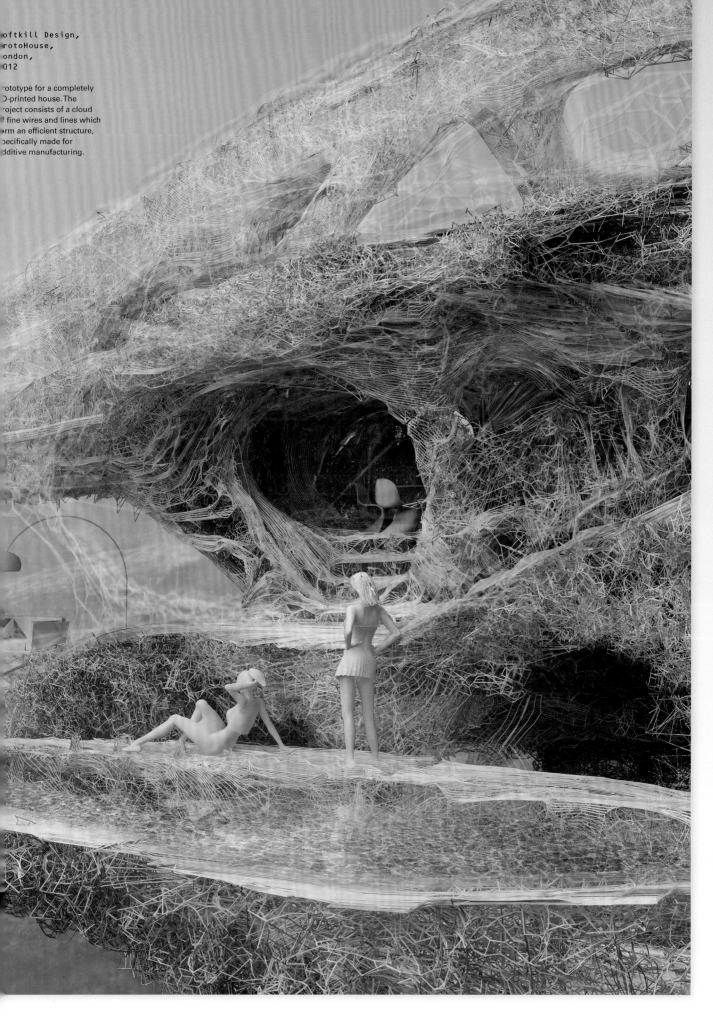

Softkill Design,
ProtoHouse,
London,
2012

Prototype for a completely
3D-printed house. The
project consists of a cloud
of fine wires and lines which
form an efficient structure,
specifically made for
additive manufacturing.

The current stage of the digital discourse is often described as 'post-digital'. Rather than mere technical arguments, a certain maturity in the discourse has given rise to new discussions about aesthetics, affects and sensations. The emphasis shifts from process to the final object and its qualities. The object is delimited and defined by a surface, often richly articulated, textured, complex or carved out. The surface produces an edge, boundary or figure defining the object. Sometimes this surface is voluptuous and smooth, sometimes rippled and irregular, sometimes in tension, sometimes loose. But what if we don't surrender to the surface and its topological, wholifying impetus? The work of Gilles Retsin Architecture is up for something else, something raw. It is not interested in the surface of the object, but in the qualities, aesthetics and moods emerging from the

Gilles Retsin
Architecture,
Guggenheim museum,
Helsinki, 2014

above: The museum explores the idea of assembling highly detailed structures out of simple linear elements, with a high degree of standardisation. Heterogeneity and variation emerge from the differentiated organisation of low-grade timber strands.

below: The building is of a raw quality – both in terms of digital organisation and materiality.

computational assembly of parts – the part-to-whole structure or mereology of the object. No overcooked soup or stew, but a plate filled with distinct, raw ingredients.

Something Else:
Softkill ProtoHouse and Guggenheim Helsinki

The idea of resisting the surface was first explored with the Softkill ProtoHouse (2012), a prototype for a 3D-printed house. An algorithm organises thousands of thin lines into stiff, interconnected structures, aligned on principal directions of stress, similar to the way fibrous structures in bone are created. The architectural consequences are fundamental: there is no more solid mass, no more topology, and no more surface. A volume is defined, not with surface but with packs of lines.

o understand the architectural effects of these
olumetric organisations, the German word
uflösung is helpful. *Auflösung* means at the
ame time 'adding resolution' and 'dissolving'.
hrough adding resolution, mass dissolves, and
ith it the known architectural modus operandi
f surface, boundary and figure. Unlimited by
ctonic constraints, the ProtoHouse allowed for
ontinuous, free variation in the organisation of
aterial. A subsequent series of projects speculate
n the consequences of the ProtoHouse in a more
ctonic reality, bound by economies of scale,
rialisation and prefabrication. The Guggenheim
useum in Helsinki (2014) introduces precise
ctonic constraints based on serialisation and
epetition, shifting the continuous variation of the
rotoHouse into a more raw state. Computational

logics of abstract organisation and disposition are
confronted with raw building elements – made of
timber, concrete or stone. Continuous and smooth
transitions make place for sudden shifts and breaks;
the columns, floor slabs and roof structure all operate
as autonomous entities with their own tectonic logics.

Something Raw:
Blokhut, HexStrata and Diamond Strata
More recent projects of the office push the logics
of discreteness to its limits, resulting in bold and
coarse digital structures. A project like Blokhut
(2015) attempts to construct an entire building with
just one building block – similar to a bit as a unit
of computation. Its raw structure is fundamentally
digital, and almost primitive. In HexStrata (2015)
and Diamond Strata (2016), a series of strands are

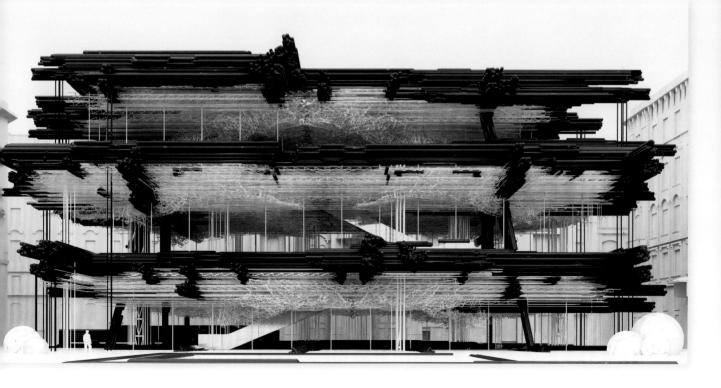

assembled into diffused, volumetric and porous slabs. While the architectural moves are bold and harsh, the figure of the building remains uncertain and diffused. The Diamond Strata project gives rise to an extreme digital structure where only the core of the architecture is left, the bare bone. There are no smooth surfaces, no subtle perforations or fragile ornaments, no delicate patterns. A single building block builds stratified slabs, which can abruptly change into columns or beams. The disposition of discrete building blocks is precise and sharp, yet messy and open ended in its aggregation.

Gilles Retsin Architecture, Diamond Strata, Multi-Family House, Belgium, 2016

above: Diamond Strata is made of volumetric linear elements with a male–female connection, establishing a digital material organisation.

below: The raw, digital logic underlying the project is based on the interaction and assembly of a single piece. A single building block constructs columns, floors, beams and ceiling.

opposite: The building block has three different hierarchical scales. The elements with the biggest scale act as the main structure.

Towards a New Spatial Experience

The consequences of the absence of surface and topology give rise to a new kind of, radically different and unknown spatial experience. This raw architecture has no more facade, no interior, no exterior, no difference between floor, column or ceiling – just the digital organisation of a single piece of matter. Rather than through surface, atmosphere is now controlled and modulated through the organisation of elementary pieces, assembled in non-topological, volumetric masses. ᴧ

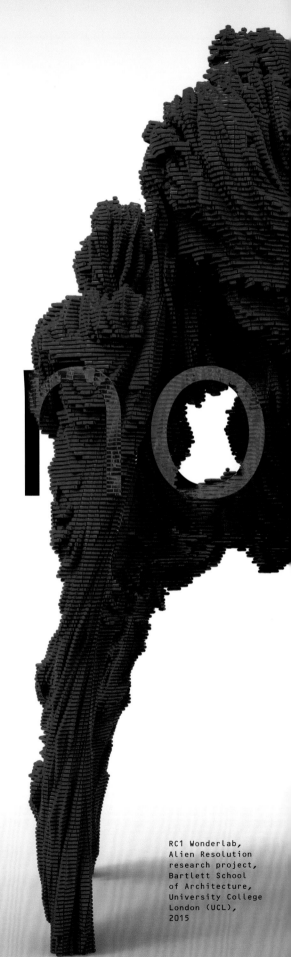

Xeno

In the Mood

RC1 Wonderlab,
Alien Resolution
research project,
Bartlett School
of Architecture,
University College
London (UCL),
2015

Alisa Andrasek

Cells

for the Unseen

ien resolution' (extremely
gh resolution of detail) was
plied to various design
plorations at the scale of
rniture and architecture.
own is a chair derived from
e process of cellular division
d local micro-gravity forces.

Forces that were previously invisible to the human eye are now being materialised in new aesthetics made possible by algorithmic design. The aptly named Wonderlab studio at University College London's Bartlett School of Architecture is running an ongoing research programme on these awe-inspiring possibilities. Its XenoCells project uses a cell division algorithm that can be applied in varying resolutions, to vastly different effect – achieving 3D-printed forms that range from sharp crystalline structures to organic folds reminiscent of internal organs. **Alisa Andrasek**, director of Wonderlab, explains.

RC1 Wonderlab,
Alien Resolution research project,
Bartlett School of Architecture,
University College London (UCL),
2015

Simulation of the topological evolution process of cellular division. Shown are 5 million cells forming intricate folds reminiscent of similar features found in internal organs. Simulation is conducted using parallel programming (GPGPU based on CUDA) allowing extremely high resolution.

The ethereal qualities of XenoCells would not be possible without the nonhuman agency that goes into the automation layers of its design and fabrication. The differentiating powers of the cell division algorithm,[1] simulating biological processes such as morphogenesis or the growth of cancer cells, create an intricate, heterogeneous and alien design vocabulary. When it is run in low resolution, polygonal, sharp-edged cells quickly generate complex structures reminiscent of crystals; while when the same algorithm is applied to a higher cellular population (that is, a greater number of building blocks within the same volume), the organic folds found in internal organs, corals and plants begin to emerge. In this project,[2] the focus was on counterintuitive architectural atmospheres, whereby extremely large and therefore 'alien' resolution is applied to the design of familiar furniture objects such as chairs, and architectural elements such as columns. The unseen is unveiled through the application of algorithms at a very 'high resolution', and this strangeness is highlighted within the context of a familiar type of design object.

XenoCells is part of the ongoing research by Wonderlab at University College London's Bartlett School of Architecture in its search for and materialisation of the rare, the unseen and the unexplored. Technological and scientific resources are expanding the reach of the phenomenal – that which is perceived by the senses – by including imperceptible entities, resulting in a new strangeness of emerging effects. The accelerated enhancement of phenomenal human perception is now possible through the noumenal – that which is perceived by the mind – operating beyond the limited processing capacity of human cognition. The consequent aesthetic power of newly found wonder and awe can now be analysed, synthesised, engineered and designed, resulting in strange moods of the unseen: novel aesthetics which reveal and materialise forces (friction, fluid dynamics and the like) that are normally hidden from human perception.

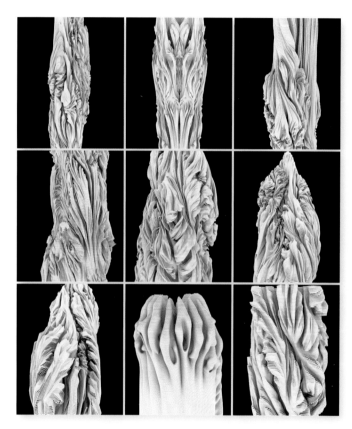

isa Andrasek with Wonderlab,
noCells,
xo-Evolution' exhibition,
M|Center for Art and Media,
rlsruhe,
15

ove: A 2.3-metre (7.5-foot) tall lumn robotically 3D printed multiple materials. The iation of the column fabric a result of the resolution of rication, where material and nstructability constraints create aesthetic effects.

above right: Column samples based on cellular division simulation. The rich diversity of possible design outcomes echoes the similar diversity this process produces in nature. The system is supersensitive to minute changes and therefore demands nonhuman assistance in the design process.

Deep data
is being
embraced
by human
sensibility,
sculpting new
cognition.

Above and right: The geometry
of the intricate folds of the
column is mathematically
programmed to adapt to the
constraints of the printing
process, but also to increase
reflection/refraction of the
column fabric and its structural
integrity.

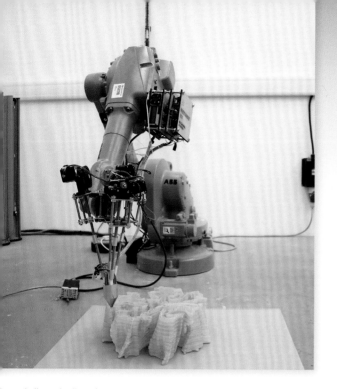

...stom-built nozzle allows for large-scale multi-
...aterial effects that are currently seen only in smaller
...achines and slower processes of 3D printing.

...e material effects of XenoCells are elusive; colour
...s depth and ambiguity, and transparency and colour
...riation create a dynamic material experience when
...nt moves through the fabric or the observer moves
...ound it.

However, design explorations at such a high volume of data exceed the human capacity to 'search' for possible designs. There is an increasing necessity for 'design assistance' via the automation of the design process, where recent developments in artificial intelligence and deep learning can be applied to 'accelerate' design. This agency beyond the human, together with unprecedentedly high resolutions, is yielding truly alien moods, with novel aesthetics, but is also changing the nature of the design process itself. Synthesised computational methods are making ever greater tasks achievable in ever shorter periods, essentially speeding up human time.[3]

The automation of construction, such as robotic 3D printing, allows for the materialisation of high-resolution designs, reaching previously unimaginable levels of performance and simultaneously uncovering previously unseen aesthetic phenomena. In the XenoCells project, when attempting to 3D print the column via multi-material robotic extrusion, the resolution of the design was multiple orders higher than what could be currently printed. Instead of lowering it, the research team stepped it up, which through densification changed the mineral geometry into intricate organic wrinkles. The resulting XenoCells column is ethereal, with the materiality of robotic extrusion imprinted into it, hovering between the extreme accuracy of automated fabrication and material noise. Transitions from one material to another are blurred as a result of the nonlinearity of material heating during the printing process. The column shimmers like a crystal, its folds reminiscent of the complex wrinkling of internal organs. Biology and crystals, human and alien, revealing of the unseen …

The forthcoming meteorology of architectural atmospheres is unseen, since never before have designers had access to the scale of dust particles or algorithmic profiles of matter. Nor was there previously an artificial intelligence part of the process, evolving at the accelerated pace of computational time. Design is increasingly malleable, plastic and intricate, primed for super-performance and unseen aesthetics. It echoes the complexity found in natural formations, but also emergent phenomena stemming from its underlying abstractions. The design process is performed beyond the human realm, by dipping human and artificial cognition into the ocean of billions of data particles. Noise is the new normative aesthetic, and pattern recognition is the new design method. Artificial intelligence is being applied directly to the core of creativity. Deep data is being embraced by human sensibility, sculpting new cognition. The emerging mood is one of the unseen. ⌂

Notes
1. Andy Lomas, 'Cellular Forms: An Artistic Exploration of Morphogenesis', undated, http://www.andylomas.com/extra/andylomas_paper_cellular_forms_aisb50.pdf.
2. Wonderlab's study 'Alien Within the Familiar' preceded XenoCells, with students Ningzhu Wang, Jong Hee Lee, Zhong Danli, Feng Zhou, directed by Alisa Andrasek and Daghan Cam.
3. See Mario Carpo, 'Breaking the Curve', *Artforum*, February 2014, pp 169–73.

Benjamin H Bratton

BAD MOOD

'Boring cloud':
self-storage facility,
Los Angeles,
2015

ON DESIGN AND 'EMPATHY'

'Boring knife':
residential high-rises,
Budapest,
2015

Evocative design is not only concerned with enriching our experience of our environment: it can also be used to seduce us into consuming. Empathy is as crucial to this strategy of entrapment as it is to designing with more magnanimous aims in mind. **Benjamin H Bratton**, Professor of Visual Arts and Director of the Center for Design and Geopolitics at the University of California, San Diego, reflects on the matter, and considers whether the moodlessness that defines seemingly empathy-free design is necessarily a bad thing.

'Boring sign':
near Joshua Tree,
California,
2008

nvironments tuned to create mood may be well tuned
badly tuned, calming or cloying, but what about an
rchitecture of and for 'moodlessness'? For whom (or what)
it possible, and when? Is it just a matter of affectlessness
of zeroed-out emotion – or something more cunning? Is it
nother kind of performance (or respite from them?). Surely
e enactment of emotion is a crucial evolutionary strategy for
telligent social species (including companion species). Being
te, graceful, fearful, seductive are all ways that creatures
terrelate. Mood could even be defined as the cumulative
motional and experiential resonance of these interrelations
a given moment. If so, is moodlessness merely the absence
those interrelations, or instead is it a particular sort of
terrelation: is boredom, for example, a mood or is it the
sence of mood?

As our global modernities build vast logistical
chipelagos – factories, warehouses, container ships,
stribution routes, switching depots – all briefly inhabited by
animate objects in passing, it could be said that we already
ve a contemporary moodless architecture, in that those
ssing objects are incapable of emotion in any normal sense.
et we build so many houses for them. Perhaps the reasons
r this are stranger, more contradictory and more instructive
an we realise?

This short essay considers a few entry points
to the strange problems posed for the design of mood,
oodfulness and moodlessness. It will orbit the specific
ale and temporality of architecture, but will depart to and
om that station in doing so. Evidentiary inferences include:

Boring New Promise Land':
office complex near the
Mojave Air and Space Port,
Mojave,
California,
2015

Muzak, gastronomy, data centres, industrial zones, branded
retail, artificial intelligence, child-faced dogs and dog-faced
children, depression, burnt affect, seed banks, virtual reality
platforms, and the philosophical and practical importance
of disenchantment and disillusion. My intention, in short,
is to complicate the role of a particular mood – empathy
– and to challenge the role played by the cynical/earnest
performance of empathy and of 'empathiness': the mood
that this performance may create by design (or for designers)
independent of any actual empathy at work.

EXHIBITIONS OF EMPATHY

It has been suggested that the killer social application of
virtual reality is empathy; being able to step inside the virtual
shoes of another person or creature promises, for some, a
new general pedagogy. But what about 'reality reality'? Is it
full of empathy gaps, and if so where are they? Is empathy
something exceptional to normal social interdependence or is
it a core function thereof? For example, as already hinted, the
capacity to be 'cute' is a fine strategy for evolutionary success.
It draws two creatures together in a performance of emphatic
recognition and response, irrespective of any actual mutual
identification. The cute thing stares up at you with big Keane
child eyes and so you give it surplus food. This is, as we know,
a basic protocol of the mutual domestication of humans and
dogs. You feel empathy for this panting half-wolf creature on
the periphery; you sense its hunger, desperation and most of
all gratitude for your kindness, though much of this may all
be in your head. Dogs' faces, nevertheless, are selected thereby
to evolve in relation to how well they serve to flatter the
experience of empathetic obligation and self-satisfaction that
the most precious of them would trigger in us.

While this particular cute-empathy dynamic is not some Lamarckian plot by dogs (we presume), other economies do operate on the deliberate performance of empathy and empathy-inducement. Service design and experience design hinge not only on smooth user-facing processes, but also on setting the mood for the value-add of the personal touch. In the classic of Reagan-era American sociology, *The Managed Heart: The Commercialization of Human Feeling* (1983), Arlie Russell Hochschild shows how 'female' labour in particular – nursing, flight attending, bank telling, waitressing – demands not only the performance of an expert convenience, but an additional emotional work of making customers feel like the employee (and the company by proxy) truly cares about their predicament, not just in transactional terms, but on a human one-to-one level, 117 times per hour.[1] The enforcement of that emotional performance is also a managerial responsibility: What does it say about someone who just does the bare minimum? Don't you really love your job? Why weren't you at the mindfulness workshop?

The performance of empathy is even expected of machine intelligence. The Turing Test depends on similar back-and-forth demands. The AI must not only be intelligent in some transistor-embodied way, it must convince a human that it thinks like humans do. Unless it can coax empathy from the human, it may not be recognised as intelligent, and may even be switched off (wolves solved this test several thousand years ago). An advanced AI will observe that empathetic species, like dolphins and pandas, receive stronger protection against extinction than more ecologically crucial species that cannot smile. Is this why interim AIs, such as 'assistants' Cortana, Alexa and Siri have default 'female' voices instead of the deep tone of the creepily calm/passive aggressive HAL 9000?

'Boring Internet':
conference attendees
visiting a data centre
near Princeton,
New Jersey,
2014

EATING MOODY SPACE

As empathy is deliberately performed to ensure particular affects, it is also a strategy of and for mood-making design. It is one way that designers might seek to entice or enrol users or clients into the worlds, systems, scenarios and functions on the menu.

In the seams that bind industrial design, cognitive science and experience design, for example, that a designer should empathise with the user is an axiomatic commandment. Its pedagogy may instil in acolytes the need to 'be passionate' about empathy in and of itself. For this discourse, bad design may be the work of 'engineers', defined as those who pay too much attention to how systems work and not enough to how regular people interpret them, or it may be the fault of bad designers, chiefly those self-satisfied with creating beautiful, impractical signature works.[2]

In architectural seminars and studios, empathy and empathy tropes have a similar currency. 'Social practice' designers will often preface or frame their work with recitations on the importance of listening, collaboration, communication, dialogue, understanding, a lack of hierarchy in procedural ambition, and the methodological suspension of any authorial design expertise for as long as possible. Indeed, empathy is often presented as if it *were* design expertise, and vice versa. Following on from the evolutionary importance of cuteness for how animals and children secure food from those in whose care they find themselves, we also observe that many such design practices will use childlike stylistic elements in the demonstration of the proposal or project: bright primary colours, ukulele pop, crayon fonts, children's handprints, and the over-determined participation of now-again-infantile senior citizen stakeholders. That the eventual design plan ends up replicating an exact formula of vernacular materials and mixed-use everything – suggesting that no participatory discovery-phase design research was even necessary in the first place – does not discourage many practices from ensuring a project's success by over-modelling empathy-as-service. It works.

'Boring flight':
passenger from
California to Japan,
over Pacific Ocean,
2016

ther practices may articulate empathy tropes not to flatter
e participation of constituents on moral terms, but rather
demonstrate alignment with a client's business goals.
randed retail theatres' – for sneakers, electronics, cars and,
pecially, art – are an urban real-estate genre underwritten
the promise that the translation of a brand's strategic
pathy with a target psychodemographic can be conveyed
the mood composed by critical connoisseurship. The more
ecise the mood, the more clearly the brand is felt to 'get it'.
otels, restaurants and Disney have made this design principle
entral investment for many years, but now the logistical
complishments of ecommerce have made retail experience
sign a more general and mandatory concern, from one end
the shopping district to the other.

e ante is upped by cult projects like Café Gratitude, where
t only must the staff pretend to like you and to enjoy
rving you, the customers too are expected (even required)
make a declaration of spiritual solidarity with this elective
opian community of lunch-goers. In order to get food, you
der out loud plates named 'I Am Gracious', 'I Am Devoted'
'I Am Liberated'. For a brand built on sophistry and
lipsism, casting everything in the first-person singular such
at important states of being could be called upon just by
ying so, is one apotheosis of empathetic user-centred design.[3]

deed, this slippage between work-as-emotional performance
d shopping-as-emotional work is perhaps one of its
during accomplishments, and its diverse history is not just
matter for retail architectures.[4] Sound is also crucial to how
od is set, not just by acoustics, but by how the soundtrack
a location's virtual cinema is properly supportive of the
ended ambience. After Erik Satie's 'furniture music' and
fore Brian Eno's 'Ambient' music, the Muzak corporation
bed soothing and barely perceptible mood sounds into the
ices, elevators and malls of 20th-century America – even
ndon B Johnson's White House. By design, listeners would
guided almost subliminally through their working day by

'Boring transparency':
revolving glass doors,
near London,
2008

'stimulus progression' algorithms that were to make them
calm, energetic, focused or relaxed at just the right time.[5] If
we suspend disbelief just so, we see how setting an ideal mood
for the work space and setting an ideal mood for shopping
and leisure space entail the same techniques.

My examples all involve strategic empathy as a fundamental
design rationale, but how they do this is not identical.
Whereas one may explicitly perform empathy in a winking
manner (branded retail), another may obscure it from the
worker/shopper (Muzak), and another may perform it for
the client(s) through implications about how design will
connect end-users (social practice). Elsewhere, the gig/sharing
economy opens up new pathways for confluence, including
paying neighbours to work for you, drive for you and, at least
as much as shopping means choosing and getting things and
bringing them to your house, to shop for you as well. Some of
us may want to take the work out of leisure by subcontracting
it to someone else. Virtual-reality-as-empathy takes on a new
meaning if even flâneuring the mall could be learned through
job simulator applications. In such scenarios, an architecture
without mood, one that makes no demands for experiential
labour, may be a welcome relief.

'Boring cabbage and
fire extinguisher':
La Jolla, California
and Tokyo,
2016

'Boring sleep':
Heathrow Airport,
London,
2016

(NOT) DESIGNING TRAPS

My conclusions about empathy and its various performances are congruent with Benedict Singleton's identification of something even more fundamental: all design is the design of 'traps'.[6] It traps users in a just-so way towards just-so ends. That is, design is a plot, and to design is to plot. To design a trap, one must have sufficient empathy with whatever is to be trapped; you must think like a fox, bear or customer in order to know how to get that creature to come or go as you intend. Too little empathy and you miscalculate means; too much empathy and you miscalculate ends. Religious architectures of various sorts have, for example, developed an expertise in balancing revelation and occlusion, symmetry and volume, legibility and line-of-sight, mystery and mastery. Such balance enables this genre – sacred spaces predicated on the empathies of predation and its atonement – to secure its own food supply: namely, people and their beliefs (and their beliefs about their beliefs).

My perspective on the problematics and opportunities of mood and architecture may, however, be at odds with some other design theories. Some argue that its affect is what architecture does; ultimately, affect is the only function, not the retroactive diagrammatics that pass for functionalism. Others may ponder the medieval spookiness of the object (or of the nominal category 'object') and argue that a metaphysical unknowability of singularly self-subtracted assemblages underwrites a special kind of architecture that does not do anything per se but just is. We sometimes even hear both misapprehensions spoken simultaneously.[7] Between the two are claims that feel like they straddle both (even if they are logically validated by neither). It is suggested that one should design architecture as if it existed on an ontological plane of absolute discreetness, but should also take time to savour its formal 'formliness' (without all the urbanism baggage) because good form is delicious and/but because objects ultimately have no relations (only qualities, including being sweet, sour or kawaii, which are somehow non-relational). That is, we are to be at once in awe of the object that is withdrawn from us into metaphysical otherness – as all objects supposedly are, but which special formalist objects are especially – and we are also to be drawn into an intense emotional, nervous perceptional relationship with that object and its affects (or, as it was put, to 'love' it).[8]

Perhaps what we read in this symptomatic confusion is design's bad-faith relationship to its own economies of empathy and trapping (even of and for itself). Perhaps the designer's empathy with the designed (that is, with the object or with the user) becomes just too much to bear, especially its performative demands. The work of design-as-empathy/empathy-as-design is emotionally exhausting, taxing, even deadening. If some designers want to let the thing just be and to pause all the cynical earnestness for a moment, then can we blame them for it? (This may also speak to architecture's famously opportunistic relationship to 'theory' and the tendency to borrow concepts half-chewed and deploy them resourcefully. To me, a 'design theorist', this is fine. Opportunists innovate on what they steal, whereas the faithful weaponise concepts as a matter of duty: give me the former any day.) If one impetus to make things that just are is born from a fatigue with conjuring illusory publics – by making sorrowful eyes, singing songs, empathising with logistical niceties as if they were magical, mobilising clients' product lifecycle plans towards crowd control – then this interest deserves a better and more contemporary design philosophy of the object than what it has in hand.

'Boring self-portrait':
test of LiDAR system,
San Francisco,
2015

Perhaps the rainbow pangs invested in obscure claims for the categorical qualities of the word 'object' are in response to how those claims, however unlikely it may be, nevertheless provide images of thought that, for some, feel good to design with. However matched or mismatched they may be with what eventually emerges, the vocabulary seems empathetic to the frustrations of some very talented designers. Even a dull and inadequate philosophy of design can function (relationally) as a theoretical mood with which to reframe design work, and as a slang with which to refuse some of its emotional demands. The eventual resignation that the original theoretical apparatus may bear so little resemblance to what is designed in its name is a secondary disenchantment deferrable to a latter time.

In other words, how do you build a trap to catch a trap-builder? Tell them, empathetically, that they are not building a trap at all. ᗺ

Notes

1. Arlie Russell Hochschild, *The Managed Heart: Commercialization of Human Feeling*, University of California Press (Berkeley, CA), 1983.
2. Donald A Norman, *Emotional Design: Why We Love (or Hate) Everyday Things*, Basic Books (New York), 2005.
3. *Ibid.*
4. For a lively history, see Norman A Klein, *The Vatican to Vegas: A History of Special Effects*, New Press (New York), 2004.
5. On Muzak, see Joseph Lanza, *Elevator Music: A Surreal History of Muzak, Easy-Listening, and Other Moodsong*, University of Michigan Press (Ann Arbor, MI), 2004, and *Blue Monday: Stories of Absurd Realities and Natural Philosophies*, Actar (Barcelona), 2007.
6. Benedict Singleton, '(Notes Toward) Speculative Design', in Robin Mackay, Luke Pendrell and James Trafford (eds), *Speculative Aesthetics*, Urbanomic Press (Falmouth), 2014.
7. To hear both misapprehensions in equal measure, listen to Graham Harman's lecture and Mark Foster Gage's response at Syracuse University School of Architecture, 25 September 2014: https://soa.svr.edu/live/events/74-graham-harman-with-mark-gage.
8. *Ibid*, Gage's remarks.

'Boring droids versus clones':
Star Wars miniatures,
Legoland, Carlsbad,
California,
2016

Emanating
Objects

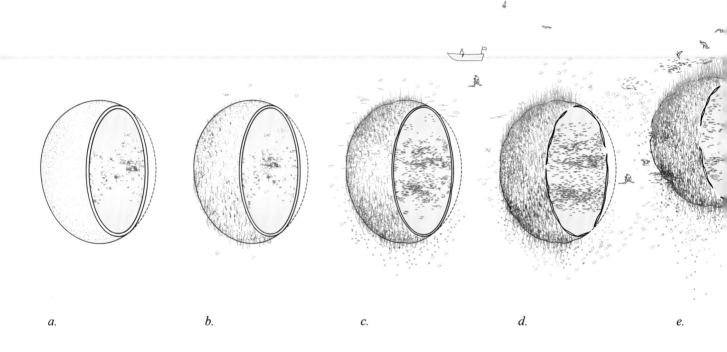

a.   b.   c.   d.   e.

The Bittertang Farm,
Gelatinous Orb –
The Ocean,
2009

Throughout the orb's lifespan its form will
continuously transform to create thickened
spatial regions around its perimeter as plants
and animals gravitate towards it.

Michael Loverich

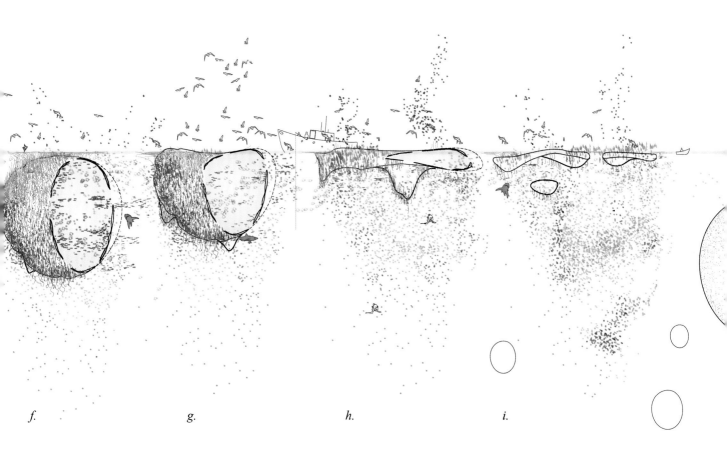

f. *g.* *h.* *i.*

The Atmospheric Ecosystems Generated
by Gelatinous Orb and Buru Buru

The Bittertang Farm is a New York-based experimental design firm that strives to bring happiness into the built environment by exploring the pleasurable, frothy features of the world around us. **Michael Loverich**, who cofounded the practice together with Antonio Torres, here describes two of its interventions. Taking the form of fantastical narrative ecosystems, they inspire new experiential moods.

The Bittertang Farm,
Gelatinous Orb –
The Ocean,
2009

Once set loose in the wild, the orb will literally take on a life of its own, following currents and attracting living entities wherever it goes, possibly even mingling with other spheres of various ages, sharing their ecosystems and giving them away as they collapse and die.

The orb will not only be a productive and efficient farm; the giant spherical reefs will become an aestheticised and living object to be explored by divers and recreational fisherman. Shape and gelatin mixture will produce different living conditions and various reef typologies: no two will be the same.

e orb is made of gelatin, which
ts climax state will take on a
netary quality as it supports
merous plants and animals,
stratified according to their
owing requirements.

Within folklore, environments are used to create specific moods. When successful they transport the listener to an alternative world. Forests are often enchanted or haunted and their formal descriptions are detailed to the point that they become the supporting characters within the narration. *Hänsel and Gretel* is nothing without the aesthetics of the dense impenetrable woods or the descriptions of the way the two siblings navigate that forest and interact with the creatures that inhabit it. Out of this comes a narrative ecosystem; the interaction of living and non-living elements is what creates the story's mood. Creepiness is not explicitly stated, but is built into the story through the detailed development of how the characters interact as part of this ecosystem.

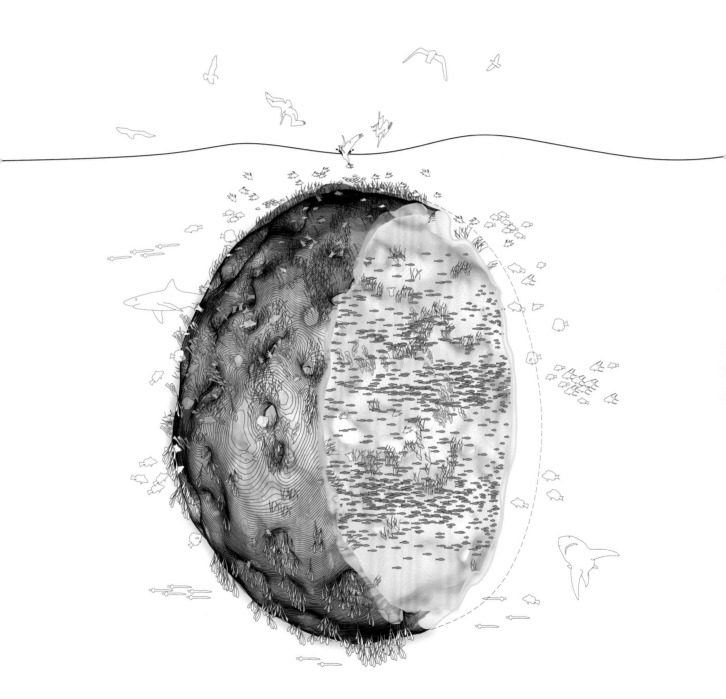

By designing real or fantastical ecosystems for architectural interventions, new experiential moods can be created. In The Bittertang Farm's Gelatinous Orb project, the main character is the ocean, which provides a different world to that of the terrestrial, and often a terrifying one. To be immersed in liquid is to be immersed in colour, in living matter, a place where gravity seems to weaken and where one could quickly drown. In the vast ocean it is not a matter of making space for life, but making objects that attract life. In this case the object is a gelatin orb.

Orbs on land are merely balls; however, orbs in the water are planetary because they can be accessed and experienced on all sides. This planetary quality is enhanced through the encrustation of living matter in the form of algae, seaweed and molluscs across the orb's surface, and their natural tendency to stratify by variety based on growing requirements. The ecological particulate that surrounds the orb could be viewed as a physical re-creation of an aura, but more importantly it produces dense, dynamic spatial conditions capable of generating and sustaining life. This particulate produces an ever-evolving form with its own temporality, its own lifespan, its own climactic effects, and its own behaviours existing outside of the man-made and controlled. It is ominous when it is a wild entity floating freely throughout the expansive oceans, seemingly in control of itself.

The Bittertang Farm,
Buru Buru,
Ragdale,
Lake Forest,
Illinois,
2014

below middle: Buru Buru's approach is non-frontal and accessed from the oblique. By exposing the amphitheatre's mo massive face it obscures any reading of its inner contents and programme.

below bottom: The stage is sheltered by the organic mound, creating an understorey space that opens up to the seating area Hay wattles hang over the stage, seeded with vines, they thicken the understorey.

Buru Buru exists in a secluded bucolic prairie, a setting where hay is commonly seen; however, here it is used in an unfamiliar manner, fluctuating between the bodily and the pastoral rather than the agrarian. Buru Buru's environment, as opposed to Gelatinous Orbs, is non-threatening, so the project explores more complex forms and structures. At times the presence of a body can be sensed within the turgid, twisting forms of the sausages (are those legs or belly rolls?), or at a larger scale emanating from the steaming and decomposing mass reminiscent of the secretions from a giant creature who recently vacated the scene.

The seclusion of the site means it is encountered rarely and only by small parties who stumble across its path, feeling as though they might have disturbed it. It does not therefore gain an identity like architecture usually does, through being seen in use or in its recognisable form, but instead through a startled interaction and an individualised exploration of form and behaviour. Built of hay and exposed to the elements, at any moment it could be sweating, steaming, desiccating and exfoliating. It is constantly rotting and sprouting new life, producing a physical aura as it off-gasses. Insects and birds are attracted to it, flying and buzzing around it to produce a visual aroma. These elements, as well as the way Buru Buru is found and experienced, contribute to the architecture's form and ecosystem, defining the mood of all events that occur within its presence. ∆

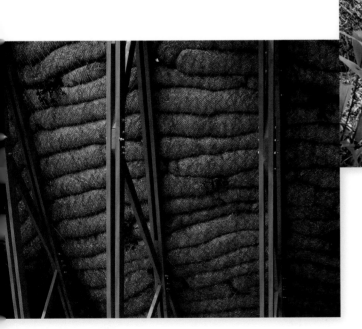

Eric Goldemberg

Mood, Posture

and
Rhythmic
Feedback

MONAD Studio's Sonic Experiments with 3D-Printed Musical Instruments

Engaging with physical sensations is a primary method of transmitting mood through design. Based in North Miami Beach, Florida, design research practice MONAD Studio has been collaborating with musicians, composers and luthiers to explore new paths for architecture where aural, visual and tactile stimuli come together. **Eric Goldemberg**, co-founder with Veronica Zalcberg of MONAD Studio, here describes the enigmatic and highly charged results of the collaboration, which use pulsation and morphology to add more sensory and even erotic dimensions to our perception of space.

Music experienced live can trigger all sorts of bodily reactions and moods that transport the mind to zones of pure sensory activity, rendering the body a conduit of multiple micro-transmitted signals of pulsating input that send shivers down a listener's spine. MONAD Studio's interest in tackling this very physical experience at the scale of the human body is coupled with design morphologies that further evoke rhythmical, intensely sonic pulses in order to create tension between the musician's postures and the prosthetic musical instruments. Architecture projects motivated by harnessing sonic mayhem through three-dimensional form represent a radical shift in practice for this Miami-based studio; a move towards the creation of material environments that cultivate feedback. A reciprocal relation between subject and object motivated by the enhancement of rhythmic moods in the perceptual field, this technique adopted from the sonic world unlocks new potentials for design to engage directly with the ever-changing postures of the human body.

Rhythmic Perception as the Generator of Moods

A close reading of contemporary design reveals sensations oozing from pulsating rhythms in the articulation of surfaces in architecture, energised by the beat surging from an increased awareness of detail within a sensibility of topological tectonics. Built examples of this design sensibility can be found in Ali Rahim and Hina Jamelle's prefabricated wall for the exhibition 'Home Delivery: Fabricating the Modern Dwelling' at the Museum of Modern Art, New York (2008), rhythmically modulated with components that effect a subjacent geometry of incremental difference. Also Michael Hansmeyer and Benjamin Dillenburger's Arabesque Wall (2015) and Digital Grotesque (2013) projects evoke styles by association in the eye of the beholder by means of iterative tiling and subdivision methods, materialised with massively 3D-printed ornamental details at the scale of millimetres.

MONAD Studio | Eric Goldemberg + Veronica Zalcberg with Scott F Hall, 2-string piezoelectric violin, Miami, 2015

previous spread: The prosthetic envelope of the violin is organised by smooth cavities and a structural lattice that intensify the rhythmic metrics of the artefact, imbuing its topology with pulsatile gestures of percussive latency.

left: Developed by MONAD Studio in collaboration with musician-luthier Scott F Hall, the 3D-printed violin is developed through digital mapping procedures that account for the variable ideal postures of the performer, which guide the formation of the architectural volume of the instrument.

MONAD Studio | Eric Goldemberg + Veronica Zalcberg
with Scott F Hall, piezoelectric monovioloncello,
Miami, 2015

This one-string cello uses piezoelectric pickups, small microphones
that are mounted to the bridge in order to transform the vibrations
of the instrument into an electric sound for further amplification or
transformation that emulate the sonic power of an electric guitar.

opposite top: Three string instruments and two wind instruments are embedded into the topological inflexions of a freestanding structure that serves as instruments rack and band shell. The field of curvilinear rhythmic gestures of the structure is disrupted by the precise placement of ergonomically designed instruments.

opposite below: The instruments' functionality in terms of sound generation has been conceived primarily by reducing an instrument family down to its barest sonic essentials. This functional minimalism, inversely, turns the design of the instrument's body interface with the human body into a musical maximalist interface for versatility of posture.

The travel bass single-stringed guitar minimal core design is supplemented with an exuberant body, and two-handed tapping technique allows articulation of notes at several times typical speed; though monophonic, the sonic illusion of complex polyphony occurs

Rhythmic effects accentuate the afterimage of detailed ornament as a trace, an index of activity registered upon architectural membranes, which codify spatial transformation and generate spatial moods. MONAD Studio is characterised by a relentless pursuit of rhythmic effects in architecture. It sets out to highlight conditions of rhythmic perception by creating spaces and artefacts that engage with our innate capacity to receive and process sensate matter that is highly articulated in series and aggregates of units that measure simultaneously space and time.

The Pulsatile Quality of Spatial Atmospheres

Given its architectural reference to motion-based spatial paradigms, the notion of pulsation creates an awareness of sensual perception related to movement, an enigmatic relationship between space and eroticism. In sex can be found the history of a cry, a rhythm, a syncope, a word wrenched from the body, scorched by *jouissance*. It is the history of the rhythms that crop up in speech well below the level of words but that constitute the history of speech, its soul, as is said of the very fine threads wound around a thousand times inside the sheath of a rope and that may break without appearing to weaken the strand. This rhythm is the intimate order of thought, its silent architecture, its main reason for being and the generator of moods.

Maurice Merleau-Ponty put it this way: 'my body and the other person's are one whole, two sides of one and the same phenomenon, and the anonymous existence of which my body is the ever-renewed trace henceforth inhabits both bodies simultaneously.'[1] These two sides of the same phenomenon cause a sequence, a musical scansion to appear; where the body begins and ends is where space begins and ends. The production of moods is about rendering this rhythm, making it give up what it has swallowed, as it were, so that the rhythm can charge the architecture.

Pulsation applies to sound and rhythm as it does to architecture, where a pulse provides a guideline for articulation, a thread to pull, which pushes back and pushes forward, a locus to navigate around and through. Rhythm appears as regulated time, governed by rational laws, but in contact with what is least rational in human being: the lived, the carnal, the body. Time and space, the cyclical and the linear, exert a reciprocal action, they measure themselves against one another; each one makes itself and is made a measuring-measure; everything is defined by cyclical repetitions through linear repetitions. Rhythm is born of moments of intensity, incommensurable accents that create unequal extensions of duration. Whereas meter presumes an even division of a uniform time, rhythm presupposes a time of flux, of multiple speeds and reversible relations that can be calibrated to define a specific spatial atmosphere.

n sex can be found the history of a cry, a rhythm, a syncope, a word wrenched from the body, scorched by *jouissance*.

Pulsation applies to
sound and rhythm as
it does to architecture

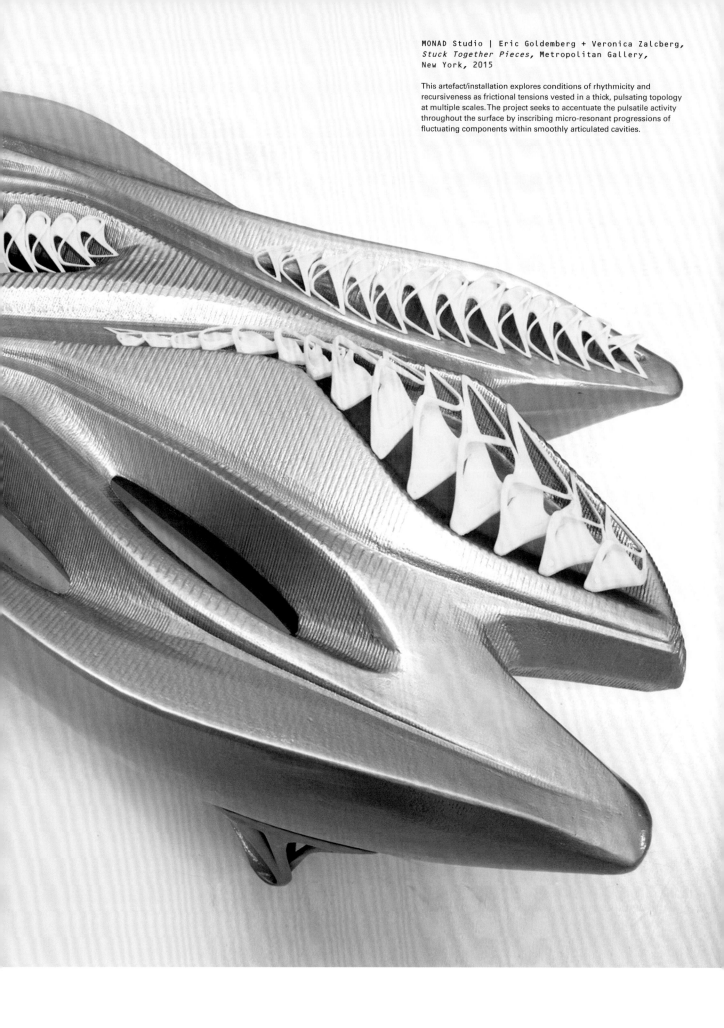

MONAD Studio | Eric Goldemberg + Veronica Zalcberg,
Stuck Together Pieces, Metropolitan Gallery,
New York, 2015

This artefact/installation explores conditions of rhythmicity and recursiveness as frictional tensions vested in a thick, pulsating topology at multiple scales. The project seeks to accentuate the pulsatile activity throughout the surface by inscribing micro-resonant progressions of fluctuating components within smoothly articulated cavities.

MONAD Studio's Architecture of Feedback

Feedback, as exemplified by the artefacts designed by MONAD Studio, is the productive exchange between posture and material organisation that can be imbued by the different moods resulting from atmospheres of pulsation. These atmospheres can be summarised through a series of distinct design categories that set the scope of operations to generate moods. The first of these categories, Accurate Emotion, refers to the precise control of form and shape in a pursuit of discipline that insists upon a clarity and precision with regard to seemingly unreasonable propositions, exerting a metric control over materials, configurations and effects that resist description. This sensibility allows architecture to deliver the impossible: contortion, a measured erotics, a surreal rigour. The second category, Animate Disruption, is interested in sensory impulse, functional distinction and imposed separation within architecture to dislocate a user, a charged programmatic relationship with an audience. This disruption is tied into a keen notion of experience and behaviour through form. Lastly, Frictional Seduction represents the obsession around behaviour and atmosphere that can be teased out within the vehicle of feedback. It is robust enough to encompass both the physical and immaterial realms.

An example of applied feedback through design strategies is MONAD Studio's *Multi* sonic installation, exhibited and performed at the Jacob Javits Center in New York in 2015. A five-piece bundle, it consists of a piezoelectric violin; monobaribasitar (travel bass guitar); piezoelectric cello; small bifurcated didgeridoo; and hornucopia (a large coiling didgeridoo, also known as a drone pipe). Three performers play live the five instruments supported by a sonic wall that serves as band shell and instruments rack. The framework itself is also another instrument that produces a drone, an emergent sonic environment to envelope the audience in moods that resonate with the pulsatile feedback of these instruments.

Feedback as the Visceral Experience of Atmosphere

> The reverberation infused into experience produced by guitar feedback is a major milestone of heavy rock music. … One can say that turning up as loud as you can and allowing the harsh feedback to envelope a crowd is the essential difference between playing a song and performing it.
> – Andrew Santa Lucia[2]

MONAD Studio's architectures act as a momentary testimony to a guttural technique of using destabilising forces in feedback within their representation, their drawings and sonic artefacts, to fundamentally move out of different stages

MONAD Studio | Eric Goldemberg + Veronica Zalcberg with Scott F Hall, hornucopian dronepipe, Miami, 2015

top: In the hornucopian, the exploration of the ergonomics of the human form and the expression of the instrument is particularly evident as the large instrument sits not on, but around the player, draping over the musician's body like an anaconda for a mutually inflective relationship.

above: The hornucopian dronepipe is a wind instrument whose morphology echoes that of strangler fig trees and is generated by the helicoidal extrusion of a bundle of tubes that alternate functions of support, sonic amplification channel and multiple handles that allow the performer to assume multiple postures.

MONAD Studio | Eric Goldemberg + Veronica Zalcberg, *Abyecto* sonic environment, Miami Beach Urban Studios, Miami, 2015

opposite: The interactive installation sets up a productive feedback network for the room, the 3D mural, the embedded guitars, the performers and the public to be involved in the shaping of a complex, collective sensorial obje

in projects and into newness – only possible by enhancing experience through a shaking-up of the foundations of perception and design. The practice's projects incorporate the fundamental reverberations implied by their physical spaces as a sort of emergent form that affects the singularity of its drawings and installations to become a project in and of itself – autonomy through codependency with reality.

Feedback fills the spaces between the forms, the notes. The first generations of electric guitarists considered feedback to be bad, a technical mishap to be avoided. Jimi Hendrix discovered ways to use it as a musical expression in its own right, glorified in his Woodstock performance of *The Star-Spangled Banner*, the moody and spacey *Pali Gap* and the war-evocative, wah-wah-infused wails in *Machine Gun*. If the amplifier is loud enough, its sound can physically shake a guitar's pickups enough to produce a current. That current gets sent to the amp, which then vibrates the pickups harder, which sends even more current to the amp, which in turn produces even more sound. This feedback loop builds rapidly, getting louder and louder. Hendrix was one of the first guitarists to think of his instrument as a way to modulate an electrical signal first and foremost. He didn't just pluck and strum the strings; he scraped them and swatted them and played with their tension. And he produced his most distinctive sounds by letting the amp itself vibrate his guitar's pickups.

Hendrix was one of the first guitarists to think of his instrument as a way to modulate an electrical signal first and foremost.

This frictional empathy between the body and the instrument can be seen in MONAD's generous folding of shape and event through rhythmic feedback that embody the actual discipline of architecture, which is a convoluted mess of outside influence, inside drawing and in-between mediations, in service of creating a proposition of characterised existence, a new atmosphere.

Through collaborations with musicians, composers and luthiers, the partners at MONAD Studio have been able to develop projects that add more dimensions and qualities to the perception of space. The resulting sonic installations and 3D-printed musical instruments activate relations that define new possible applications for architecture as a medium for the transmission of sensations. Aural, visual and tactile senses are activated by the morphology of their pieces, generating a network of social interaction that augments the role of architecture from background to active fodder for sensory activity.

The conditions of form, programme and atmosphere are staged so that sound can be produced and received as spatial experience with particular consideration for notions of posture, playing habits and the necessary ergonomic adaptations to improve existent musical instruments and create new, unprecedented ones.

The contribution of the sonic dimension to an architecture of moods is exemplified by MONAD Studio's interest in coalescing the physical sensations of the experience of music with the precisely shaped and scaled profiles of artefacts that became highly charged functional and aesthetic extensions of the body, creating an entirely new domain of design where architecture and music intersect to engender enigmatic objects of projective desire and evocative thrust. The intimate space surrounding the body is the most immediate concern for this new domain of design. Mood emerges from the oozing sensations enacted by provocative prosthetic adaptations, leading to innovative modalities of performance encoded in enigmatic, yet precise sonic architectures. ∆

Notes
1. Maurice Merleau-Ponty, *Phenomenology of Perception*, trans Colin Smith, Routledge and Kegan Paul (London), 1962, p 354.
2. Andrew Santa Lucia, 'Feedbackism', in Alejandro Schieda, *Documento Arquis de Arquitectura y Urbanismo: Universo Parametrico*, Universidad de Palermo (Buenos Aires), 2015, p 22.

Marjan Colletti

The Awesome and Capricious Language of Past, Present and Future Digital Moods

Can cultural progress be held back by linguistic limitations? Architect and educator **Marjan Colletti**, cofounder of London practice MAM-arch, examines the nouns, adjectives and adjectival compounds used by the architectural profession during the first and second digital turns. He reflects on how restricted vocabularies can cause initially forward-looking concepts to descend into the realm of doctrine and '-isms', and argues that true advancement requires constant evolution of the language employed to describe it.

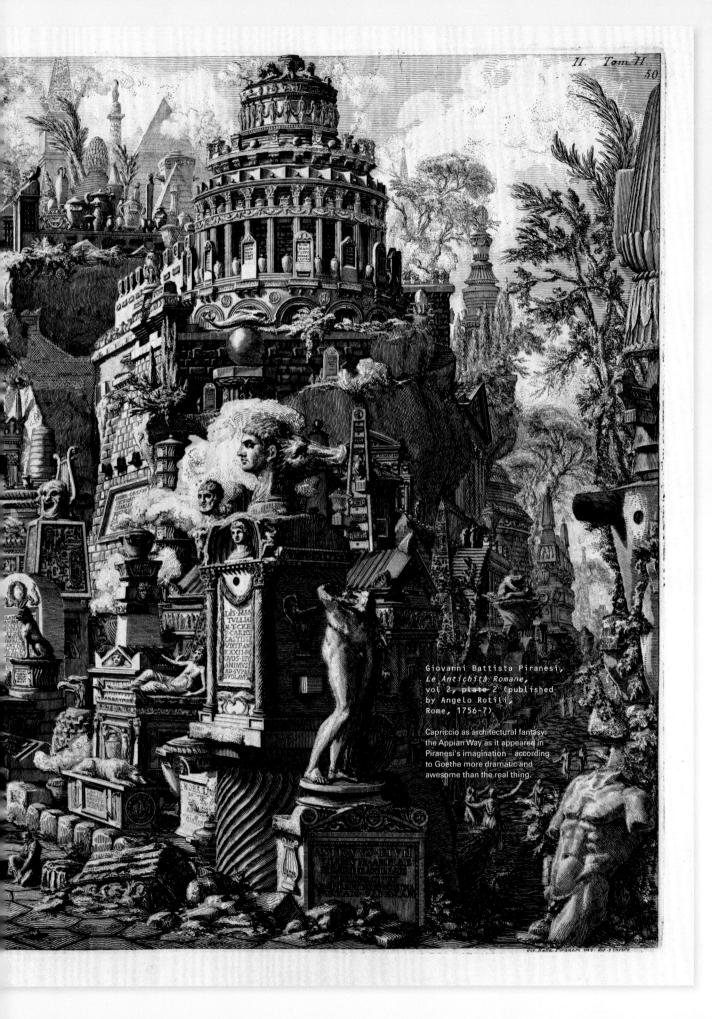

Giovanni Battista Piranesi,
Le Antichità Romane,
vol 2, plate 2 (published
by Angelo Rotili,
Rome, 1756–7)

Capriccio as architectural fantasy:
the Appian Way as it appeared in
Piranesi's imagination – according
to Goethe more dramatic and
awesome than the real thing.

The subject matter of this ⌀ provides an alluring opportunity to portray 'moods' as a powerful and yet scorned affective device for a new poetics of contemporary architecture.[1] On the one hand as some phenomenologically premeditated, and by digital tools predictable, strategic manoeuvres instilled by the architect into sophisticated design processes. On the other hand as tactics to classify and expand a past, present and future critical vocabulary inspired by, and inspiring, digital architecture. This essay will focus on the latter, since, as Adrian Forty comments in *Words and Buildings: A Vocabulary of Modern Architecture*, 'it is striking how little discussed language has been compared to architecture's other principal medium, drawing. Part of the reason for this disparity,' he continues, 'must surely be that whereas drawing is a code over which architects hold a large measure of control, their command of language will always be disputed by every other language user.' Forty, writing from the point of view of a language user, rather than a drawing maker, identifies five differences between language and drawings: drawings are exact and language is vague; language is better at signifying things and differences than drawings; language appeals to meta-language, allowing ambiguity and precision, whilst drawing sticks to object language and restricts shifted meanings; language is linear whilst drawing presents its image all at once; and finally language allows perception to happen within the mind, contrary to drawings that demand 'intellectual contortions' in order to be understood.[2]

Mood-Mapping: Temper, Climate and Modality

Since the year 2000, when *Words and Buildings* was first published, architecture has undergone a huge transformation in theory as well as in practice. On the one hand, Forty is still right: not much has changed in the sense that architects nowadays enjoy an even larger measure of control over drawing and making, and that they still have little or even lesser command of language. This despite, or rather due to, three decades of digital evolution. Radical changes undergone by drawing – for example from illustration to information – have provoked a fundamental change in language, which is mastered by few. On the other hand, it could be contested that Forty's above-mentioned differences between drawing and words are no longer valid, or accurate.

On the contrary, digital and computational drawings (the term here of course includes modelling, simulating, coding) can effortlessly convey vague, indeterminate, adaptable information; they have undoubtedly become better at defining and describing differences and variation; they are perfect for embedding meta-information with both precise and ambiguous meaning; they are ideal for time-based representations; and they can communicate complexity in a very immediate and direct way. In any case, the 'vocabulary of [eighteen] key words' Forty discusses in part two of his book – character, context, design, flexibility, form, formal, function, history, memory, nature, order, simple, space, structure, transparency, truth, type, user – no longer suffices for contemporary architectural discourse.

The term 'mood' is hereby used as a navigational tool. Linked by a thesaurus[3] to temper, climate and modality, these concepts are in turn related to discuss subject/person/individual, context/situation/milieu and method/manner/style of digital architecture.

Marjan Colletti, Guan Lee, Tea Lim and Pavlos Fereos with MArch GAD RC2 students of The Bartlett School of Architecture, aRC(2)himera, exhibited at Haus der Architektur, Graz, Austria, 2012

Goat and hedgehog: a 'monstrous' mix-up of various design approaches, from developing skin morphologies, structure anatomies and ornamental textures to coral growth scripts, steampunk aesthetics and flocking simulations.

Temper of the Past: Capricious and Awesome

One of the possibilities of translating the term 'mood' into Italian is by the word *capriccio*: a whim, a fancy, an intense desire that is stronger than mere needs.

Etymologically two roots are proposed, both linked to animal imagery: 'the first source more directly', as David Mayernik suggests, and 'the latter metaphorically; it could also be said one describes the cause, the other the effect, of a *capriccio*'.[4] In its 17th-century meaning, *capriccio* on the one hand denotes a sudden change or start of mind, influenced by *capra* (goat), associated with frisky movements, and *riccio* as 'curl'.[5] On the other hand, it relates to *riccio* as 'hedgehog' and the Latin *caput* (head), describing someone astonished, frightened or so horrified that the hair on the head would stand on end.

A critic may argue that the last three decades of digital experimental architectural production have been rather capricious in terms of words, drawings and buildings; that they resulted from computer-aided design processes and techniques that gambol overenthusiastically towards an output too fanciful in its formalist approach, too whimsical in its ornamentalism, too precipitously seduced by techniques and technologies, too erratic to comply with the current state of normativity and legislation. Or maybe simply too grotesque and horrific to a modernist mind. As an advocate of digital architecture, one ought to disagree. Furthermore, it is important to understand that such change of mind was steered, and not random! Thus, the questions at hand are: what change? How was it steered? What caused it? And what were the effects?

If Postmodern and Deconstructivist architecture achieved spatial complexity by means of collaging contrasting independent parts, the emerging geometries of becoming digital architectures liquefied. The transitions between tectonic entities melted down into continuous, smooth, liquid, fluid topologies. In this sense, yes, the change in direction was piloted by generational differentiation and rejection of the values of parental guidance. It was a *capriccio*, but a conscious, strategic one: digital design and theory never was only a fashion, but a profound paradigm change in the way architecture could be imagined, made and communicated. It was more than refreshing and exciting. What is suggested here is that if one had to describe digitality in one word (other than exuberant[6]), then one would suggest: **awesome**. In all its whimsicality. Awesome shapes, geometries, software, hardware, machines. Everything was/is awesome.

There is little doubt that 'awesome' may not be 'proper' enough a term to discuss anything serious, perish the thought of articulating a theory, or developing a style – what horror, so many people's hair would stand on end. However, it is probably one of the most misused words in the English language. First appearing, according to the *Oxford English Dictionary*, in 1598, it signified someone feeling awe, rather than inspiring it. Already in the mid-17th century it was used in its now common meaning of **very good, excellent, fun, appealing** and so on.[7] In the 1980s, the term gained momentum, especially on the US West Coast, but lost all links to awe. If in 1982 the British newspaper *The Guardian* was mocking the surfer-dude Americanism, in July 2011 the paper had used it itself in 6,457 articles. At the time of writing, the term 'awesome' has been fully embraced in the UK, reaching even India and other countries. Albeit far from being precise, accurate or specific, it has oozed into architectural use and design speak through its use in the everyday. This to the extent of becoming what Forty describes as 'critical vocabulary',

as it can convey a specific meaning but foremost a shifting 'non-meaning', similarly to the terms 'history' and 'type'.[8] Indeed, 'awesome' can be used to describe deviant and shifting conditions, i.e. both something **great** and/or something **terrible**. Despite the emphasis given since the mid-17th century to its positive meaning, it shares its etymological origin with the negative word 'awful'. Thus it seems appropriate to use as it covers a wide gamut of moods; between, for example, Ali Rahim's **elegant, beautiful, aesthetic** architecture and Hernan Diaz Alonso's **weird, horrific, grotesque** world. Hence 'awesome' (used both in its original significance of awe-inspiring and in its modern meaning of great/terrible) may turn out to be a tremendously contemporary and immediate way to portray three decades of architecture (buildings, models, processes, drawings etc) to the younger generations, who will soon be practising, teaching and theorising a hopefully even more **intelligent, smart, resilient, sustainable** or **green** architecture.

To understand digital design in all its facets and its change in moods, one needs first to understand architecture as a field of nouns – as by Forty's list of 18 key words mentioned above. Secondly, one should engage with architecture not as a static condition, but as a 'dynamic process', as Neil Leach suggests.[9] The 1990s had wide repercussions in theories of, and approaches to, cyber and digital architecture. Terms of action and of cause such as hyper, cyber, flux, events, change, motion, animation, mobility, migration, cinema, travel, virtuality, dynamism, accident, 'speciation, transvergence, allogenesis'[10] were often used. As a result, architecture attained an attributive character: for example Stephen Perrella's 'hypersurface', Marcos Novak's 'liquid architecture', Studio Zaha Hadid's 'total fluidity' or Greg Lynn's 'animate forms'.[11]

The need to describe architecture grew exponentially. By looking at some of Lynn's books' titles and subtitles we achieve an awe-inspiring list of adjectives: **affiliative, average, bent, composite, curvilinear, differential, eidetic, folded, groovy, ideal, inorganic, monstrous, multiplicitous, pliant, parasitic, probable, proto-functional, supple, viscous.**

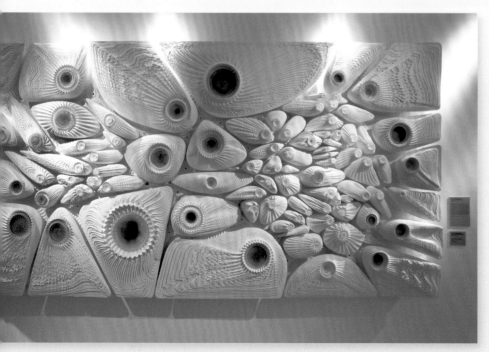

MAM-arch and Guan Lee with Richard Beckett, Algae-Cellunoi, exhibited at FRAC Centre, Orléans, France, 2013

Resilient, green, elegant and grotesque: Algae-Cellunoi is an ornamental prototype of a visible facade system that would interface architecture with nature. It is composed of a field of numerous CNCed cellular foam components with multiple patterns, gaps and crevices similar to growth layouts in sea barnacles and shells, and inserted 3D-printed flasks that host liquid algae.

With this expanded vocabulary of architecture, one may even be tempted to use more or less eccentric synonyms of awesome to make the point. For example, in chronological order: **thriven and thro** (*c* 1325), **gradely** (*c* 1400), **jelly** (*c* 1560), **topgallant, prestantious (1638), eximious (17th century), gallows (1789), budgeree (18th century), supernacular, jam/jam-up, boss (1881), fizzing, bad, deevy (1900), v.g./very good (1860s), bosker, jake, bodacious (1976), sick (US), safe (UK).**[12] To the best of my knowledge, gallows geometries or topgallant topologies have not been proposed yet.

Climate of the Present: Awesome and Second-Order Digital

Fast-forward 30 years or so, and you find digital design and architecture to have grown up into adulthood, as demonstrated by the international success of some of its protagonists. However, Mario Carpo (see article on pp 78–83) speaks of a noticeable transition from the 1990s 'cultural and technical paradigm … that defined an epoch and shaped technological change' to a new generation, a 'second digital turn' (surely a coincidence that the term 'turn' inspires twirling and therefore curling, *riccio*?); and he notes that 'The same may be happening again now. Just like the digital revolution of the 1990s (new machines, same old science) begot a new way of making, today's computational revolution (same machines, but a brand new science) is begetting a new way of thinking.'[13] Perhaps the most evident transformation has been in disrupting a strong infatuation with smoothness as theorised by Gilles Deleuze and Félix Guattari.[14] The spline has been broken; it is not awesome any more. Unsurprisingly, this second-order digitality is similarly tempered and therefore almost obliged to be capricious, especially because it is in an early teenage phase – one that notably blurs the boundaries between real and false.

In fact, compared to 30 years ago, the political, social, economic and ecological situation has changed, partly escalated. In contradiction to the mood portrayed by the theme song of the 2014 Warner Bros Pictures film *The LEGO® Movie*, not 'Everything Is Awesome'. Allow me to hazard the analogy that this film posits a relatively precise analogy to the status quo of digital architecture. Initially in the movie everything is awesome; everything is in flux, in process, cities are being built, it is all happening. Is it? Not really, as everybody is (unknowingly) following instructions to stick to the rules and avoid disorder at all costs until Emmet, an ordinary Lego construction worker prophesied to be special, is (as the film's advertising tagline puts it) 'recruited to join a quest to stop an evil tyrant from gluing the Lego universe into eternal stasis'. Every child appreciates the freedom the beloved fabricated bespoke little plastic piece can give. Surely the Lego universe is much more playful and free than envisioned by President Business and the other dogmatic master, the 'Man Upstairs', two of the movie's key protagonists? As Peter Debruge asserts in his film review, anyone who has ever played with Lego will have realised that 'a strict adherence to the rules makes for relatively mindless play, whereas things can really get fun when one dumps all the bricks onto the bedroom floor and starts freestyling creations from scratch, even if that means blending pieces from pirate, castle, space and city sets' – an approach which, he adds, President Business 'aims to quash'.[15]

Predictably, the second-order digital generation is reacting to such doom (an anagram of mood) of stasis and immobility by drawing and by language, by techniques and by vocabulary. Eventually, higher computational power, increased drawing control, theoretical speculation as well as practical knowledge demand a higher degree of drawn and linguistic definition. In his blog, François Roche (see article on pp 66–71) finds the words (the nouns) 'expertise, accuracy, performance, optimization, communication, futuristic, future, innovation, speculation, improvement, absolute, truth, parametric, post-human, positivism' very suspect relative to daily routines, suggesting other words (adjectives) as potential 'vehicles for some kind of legitimacy': **'dirty, filthy, X-rated, explicit, lewd, rude, vulgar, coarse, crude, offensive, immoral, improper, impure, off-color, degenerate, depraved, debauched, lubricious, indecent, smutty, salacious, carnal, lascivious, licentious, bawdy … but also scatological, profane, porn, skin, vile, foul, atrocious, outrageous, heinous, odious, abhorrent, abominable, disgusting, hideous, offensive, objectionable, repulsive, revolting, repellent, loathsome, nauseating, sickening, awful, dreadful, terrible, frightful and repugnant'.**[16]

A paradigmatic shift is emerging by a different logic at play, with the emergence of alternative adjectives conjoined to nouns – re-instigating and re-interpreting agency. This second-order digitality is clearly committed to articulated and deviant engagements with complex computational, physical/simulated,

Marjan Colletti, The Plantolith, exhibited in the 3D Printshow, Business Design Centre, London, 2013

Second-order digitality: a 250-kg (550-lb) 3D silica sand print that hybridises opposite geometric features of plants and monoliths. The first are growing, multi-layered, convoluted systems, whilst the latter are static, homogeneous, heavy objects. The complex geometry imitates natural processes, blurring the boundaries between tectonic elements and natural forms.

Marjan Colletti and Kadri Tamre, FrAgile 2: Porous Cast, exhibited in the Tallinn Architecture Biennale TAB 2015, Tallinn, Estonia, 2015

'It's a jungle out there': simple techniques of robotic form-carving were used to produce this prototype for a visible facade system interfacing architecture with nature. Gel inlays were employed during casting in Stewalin and bronze to achieve self-organised porosity to make the elements lighter, translucent, thermally insulating and nature-active (instigating micro-growth and insect habitat).

...o-inspired, neo-material and so on processes: **bottom-up ...rocesses, high resolution, big data, subdivided surfaces, ...xturised geometries, high articulation, extreme integration, ...ccessive design, discrete aggregations, systemic thinking, ...inimal geometries, environmental strategies, performative ...rnamentation, robotic fabrication, minimal tolerances, ...ological technologies.** Among the briefs from Unit 20 at the ...rtlett School of Architecture, University College London ...etween 2005 and 2016 were the terms: **mimetic nuclei/ ...oundaries/fields/territories, secret spaces / sacred spaces / ...blime spaces, convoluted flesh, sacred topologies / profane ...orphologies, unbalanced boundaries / undefined limits / ...ncertain edges, green paradigms in the Post-Digital Era, ...credible India, convoluted geometries / hybrid programmes ...intertwined spaces;** and the Austrian practice SOMA's book ...*ague Formations* refers variously to: **vague operations, ...robable design, fractal erosion, dilatant hysteresis, porous ...xpansion, rhizomatic bio-morphogenesis, mnemonic resonance, ...tangled strands, fibrous formations, viscous tower, ambiguous ...olidification, fibrous growth, interstitial flows, immanent ...asticity, fuzzy desires, amorphous dematerialisation, molecular ...chive, formless operations.**[17]

As Carpo states: 'It is a jungle out there, and it increasingly ...oks' – and, hearing all these terminologies proposed here, one ...ould also add: and sounds – 'like it.'[18]

Modality of the Future: Second-Order Digital and ...wesomer

...he increasingly wider and more complex glossary proposed ...re is a reflection of what second-order digital and ...mputational architects are pursuing. They – we – have ...alised that a restricted vocabulary, both in linguistic and in formal terms, is not only not contemporary, but asphyxiating and counterproductive to the advancement of the discipline. Are we not used to a Web 2.0 of an innumerable amount of information, data, categories, tags, lists, channels, trends, recommendations and suggestions? Thus it is not surprising or coincidental that one of the very first Google hits for the search 'moods' already lists an impressive inventory of possible descriptions of moods including: **accomplished, blissful, chaotic, devious, ecstatic, flirty, gloomy, hyper, indescribable, joyful, lethargic, mad, nerdy, optimistic, predatory, quixotic, relaxed, silly, touched, uncomfortable, weird.**[19]

Seen from this perspective, second-order digital experimentation in object design and spatial design merely confirms that a complex, interdisciplinary, multi-technological, cultural architectural idea must have its whimsical language and capricious childhood with all its very many moods, too, before reaching maturity. How could the protagonists of the second turn otherwise learn to understand what is relevant, what unessential; and how could they/we ever develop our own identity and their/our own interpretation of the world, with no attitude, without slang, without rebellion? Without freedom, without excess, without for example the Neo-Baroque flamboyancy of all the **289(!)** possible classifications of moods for music as provided by yet another website?[20]

Thus, the above is surely a capricious attempt to demonstrate that the future of architecture is much more varied than currently imagined and debated; beyond any current paradigms. But we can only attempt to get there if we are articulate enough to develop both the language and the drawing. And it is paramount that both do not fall back into ossified conditions of stasis, historicism and nostalgia or defaults, normativity and -isms (as in many other instances in the history of architecture, or of civilisation, any -isms end up mummified and suffocated by their own dogmas and ideologies). All the Presidents Business may have unknowingly

Marjan Colletti, Xenobaroque: Stereoscopic?, 2013

An increasingly complex and Baroque vocabulary: this design vaguely borrows from and reinterprets some of the classical ornaments and embellishments in music, such as the appoggiatura (from the Italian *appoggiare*, to lean upon), the acciaccatura (from the Italian *acciaccare*, to crush), the glissando, the Schleifer (German for slide), the trill, the mordent and the turn.

The future of architecture is much more varied than currently imagined and debated; beyond any current paradigms. But we can only attempt to get there if we are articulate enough to develop both the language and the drawing.

een instrumental in enabling the first digital era but also in lineating its end and the advent of the second digital turn d of post-digitality afterwards. Some may argue that their les were initially very constructive and even awesome in their deavour to classify and describe architecture at the end of the)th century, but that they eventually turned into a doctrine of early demarcated aesthetics and policies of words and drawing at many are finding too constrictive.

It is a recurrent pattern of history that fashions change, at aesthetic and ethical values are dismissed and overruled y other, different and partly contrary dispositions. As with ost stereotypical generational disagreements on fashion, taste, usic or references, future architects will surely dismiss this eneration's work as horrific, or childish and not yet grown-up. obody knows how long robotic fabrication, biotechnologies, ugmented reality, ubiquitous computing, the Internet of ings, systemic urbanism, energy design, advanced simulation chniques, hyper computing etc will top the charts. It is not uaranteed that architecture will be able to meet nature halfway. nd it is uncertain what the future might bring. We should accept is it not an intrinsic condition of experimental architecture be whimsically adolescent and capriciously looking for mething new, something better, something different? For mething awesomer? Some of us may certainly be in the mood r it! ∆

MAM-arch (lead designers Marjan Colletti, Marcos Cruz), Alga(e)zebo, 2012

below top: Beyond clearly demarcated aesthetics: an installation built in connection with the 2012 London Olympic celebrations which intertwines human artifice with natural surroundings in three distinct ways that grow in scale and effect. The vertical columns supporting the decorative canopy incorporate photo-bioreactors containing algae that grow and mutate when invaded by local species.

below bottom: Experimental architecture: the ornamental multifaceted patterns emulate an inverted tree silhouette, acting as a scaffold or pergola for smaller vegetation to grow into, and creating dynamic effects of light and shadows. Detail of foliage and inverted foliage.

Notes
1. Gaston Bachelard, *The Poetics of Space*, trans Maria Jolas, Beacon Press (Boston, MA), 1994 (originally published as *La poétique de l'espace*, Presses Universitaires de France (Paris), 1958).
2. Adrian Forty, *Words and Buildings: A Vocabulary of Modern Architecture*, Thames & Hudson (London), 2000, pp 14, 37–41.
3. Visuwords™: a visual thesaurus, 'Moods', http://visuwords.com/mood.
4. David Mayernik, 'The Capricci of Giovanni Paolo Panini', pp 33–41, in Lucien Steil (ed), *The Architectural Capriccio: Memory, Fantasy and Invention*, Ashgate (Farnham, UK, and Burlington, VT), 2014, p 5.
5. As suggested by the Italian saying: *ogni riccio un capriccio*, which literally translates as 'a whim for each curl'.
6. See Marjan Colletti (ed), ∆ *Exuberance: New Virtuosity in Contemporary Architecture*, March/April (no 2), 2010.
7. Robert Lane Greene, 'The Rise of "Awesome"', *Intelligent Life*, September/October 2011. In 1664 a Scottish Presbyterian sermoniser wrote that 'A sight of his cross is more awsom than the weight of it.'
8. Forty, *op cit*, p 15.
9. Neil Leach, 'Forget Heidegger', in Neil Leach (ed), *Designing For A Digital World*, Wiley-Academy (Chichester) with RIBA Future Studies (London), 2001, pp 23–6.
10. Marcos Novak, 'Speciation, Transvergence, Allogenesis: Notes on the Production of the Alien', in Neil Spiller (ed), ∆ *Reflexive Architecture*, May/June (no 3), 2002, pp 64–71.
11. Stephen Perrella, 'Hypersurface Theory: Architecture><Culture', in Giuseppa Di Cristina (ed), *Architecture and Science*, ∆ compilation, Wiley-Academy (Chichester), 2001, pp 138–47; Novak, *op cit*; Studio Zaha Hadid Institute of Architecture, Patrik Schumacher, Zaha M Hadid, *Total Fluidity: Studio Zaha Hadid, Projects 2000–2010, University of Applied Arts Vienna*, Springer (Vienna), 2011; Greg Lynn, *Animate Form*, Princeton Architectural Press (New York), 1999.
12. Oxford Dictionaries: '18 awesome ways to say awesome', 7 May 2014: http://blog.oxforddictionaries.com/2014/05/18-awesome-ways-say-awesome/. © Oxford University Press, 2014. By permission of Oxford University Press.
13. Mario Carpo, 'The Second Digital Turn', blurb for his inaugural lecture at the Bartlett School of Architecture, University College London, https://www.bartlett.ucl.ac.uk/architecture/events/mario-carpo-bartlett-ils.
14. See Gilles Deleuze and Félix Guattari, 'The Smooth and the Striated', in *A Thousand Plateaus: Capitalism and Schizophrenia*, trans. Brian Massumi, Continuum (London and New York), 1987, 2004 edn, pp 523–51.
15. Peter Debruge, 'Film Review: "The Lego Movie"', *Variety*, 2 February 2014, http://variety.com/2014/film/reviews/film-review-the-lego-movie-1201082797/.
16. François Roche, 'Stress Less, Design More', Mblog: http://blog.modelo.io/franois-roche-of-new-territories-m4-1/.
17. Kristina Schinegger and Stefan Rutzinger (eds), *Vague Operations*, Luftschacht (Vienna), 2015.
18. Mario Carpo, 'Breaking the Curve', *Artforum*, February 2014, pp 168–73.
19. http://moodlist.net/.
20. http://www.allmusic.com/moods.

The Sixth Sense

The Meaning of Atmosphere and Mood

COUNTERPOINT 06/2016 N° 244

Through its blinkered emphasis on visual form and function, has modernity divorced us from our sense of belonging to the cosmos? What, then, is the secret of creating architecture that envelops and inspires us? As scientific research increasingly favours the point of view that our unconscious – as opposed to detailed – perception has higher existential value, Helsinki-based architect and professor emeritus **Juhani Pallasmaa** argues that peripheral vision is key. Only through engagement with this can architects trigger what could be described as our sixth sense – the atmospheric.

Whether people are conscious of it or not, they actually derive countenance and sustenance from the 'atmosphere' of the things they live in or with. They are rooted in them just as a plant is in the soil in which it is planted.
— Frank Lloyd Wright, 1954[1]

Why do we identify with and feel a strong emotional attachment to certain spaces and places, while others leave us cold, or even frightened? Why do we feel like insiders and participants in some spaces, whereas in others we experience alienation and 'existential outsideness'?[2] Is this not because the settings of the first type embrace and stimulate us, make us surrender ourselves to them, and feel protected and sensually nourished, strengthening our sense of reality, belonging and self; whereas alienating and disturbing settings weaken our sense of being?

Guest-editor Matias del Campo introduces this △ with the following: 'Instead of perpetuating the techno mantra of computational design, this issue of △ strives to examine the characteristics of contemporary architectural production in terms of their ability to evoke mood, radiate atmospheric conditions and portray phenomenological traits of the sensual as well as the actual.' From this point of departure I have chosen to give certain historical and biological perspectives in order to frame the notions of mood and atmosphere in an experientially meaningful context. It is evident that modern and contemporary architectures have turned a blind eye to many of the fundamental sensory and mental issues concerning our relationships with physical settings, both 'natural' and man-made. Through modernity, the art of building has gradually focused on the technical, formal and aesthetic concerns of architecture instead of cultivating its inherent relational and mediating characteristics.

Harmony as an Architectural Aspiration

Resonance with the cosmos and a distinct proportional tuning were essential qualities of architecture from antiquity until the instrumentalised and aestheticised construction of the industrial era. The fundamental task of architecture was to create a correspondence between the

Tuning the world –
harmony of numbers in
music and architecture

Pythagoras (570–495 BC)
established the relations
between number ratios
and sound frequencies.
This woodcut shows him
experimenting with bells,
water glasses, stretched cords
and various-sized pipes. His
Hebrew counterpart, Jubal,
uses weighted hammers on an
anvil. From F Gafuro, *Theorica
musice*, 1472.

Since the
beginning of
modernity,
architectural
theory,
education and
practice have
primarily been
concerned with
the expressive
qualities of
form and
space.

Aulis Blomstedt,
Study of Pythagorean
intervals applied
to the human scale,
undated, late 1950s

Blomstedt connected visual
and musical harmonies in
a system of numbers in
accordance with Pythagorean
principles. He concluded his
meticulous studies in the
early 1960s in a proportional
system that he entitled
Canon 60.

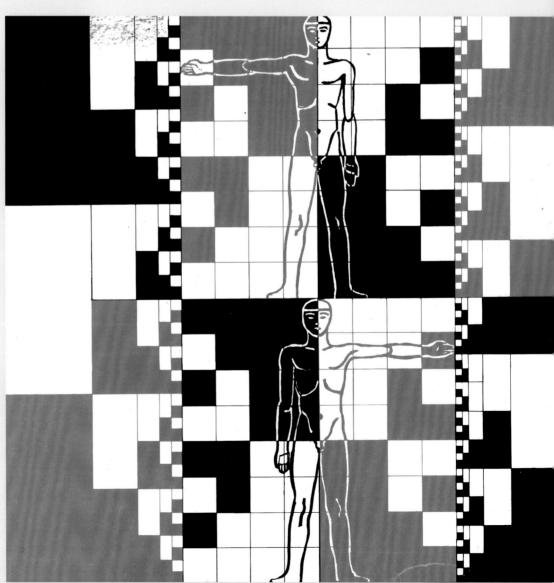

Jaakko
Klemetinpoika
Leppänen,
Petäjävesi Church,
Petäjävesi,
Finland, 1764

The intoxicating and
haptic atmosphere of an
all-wood space.

microcosm of the human realm and the macrocosm of the universe. This was sought through proportionality based on small natural numbers following Pythagorean harmonics. The Renaissance also introduced the competing proportional ideal of the Golden Section. But while during the modern era only a handful of scholars and architects, such as Hans Kayser, Rudolph Schindler, Le Corbusier and Aulis Blomstedt, were interested in proportional harmony as a means of assuring an experiential coherence of architectural works, similar to musical tuning, in today's consumerist and utilitarian society any aspiration for harmonic attunement of a larger context, or inner harmonic cohesion within the architectural work itself, has been entirely abandoned.[3]

Since the beginning of modernity, architectural theory, education and practice have primarily been concerned with the expressive qualities of form and space. Form and formal expression have even become synonymous with modernity. This orientation favours focused vision and the *Gestalt* principles described in psychological literature. Le Corbusier's credo 'Architecture is the masterly, correct and magnificent play of masses brought together in light', illustrates this visual and formal orientation.[4] Studies on vision have been primarily interested in focused perception and static gaze, which, however, are exceptional conditions in the lived reality. It is evident that focused vision necessarily implies outsideness in relation to what is seen. Thus, the fundamental experience of being embraced by space necessarily calls for diffuse and peripheral perception in motion.

It is this omnidirectional, multisensory, embodied and emotive encounter with space and place that makes us insiders and participants. I suggest, therefore, that it is the biased focusing on visual form that is responsible for the weak atmospheric quality and sense of interiority in much contemporary architecture. Architects in the modern era have considered ambiences, feelings and moods as something naive, romantic and entertaining instead of regarding such experiences as necessary constituents of environmental quality. Indeed, it is only recently that atmosphere, mood and attunement have become part of modern architectural theory and discourse.[5] Modern thinking has been interested in phenomena that can be consciously observed and rationally analysed, but the experience of mood and feeling does not arise from directed, focused and conscious attention. Mood seeps into our mental constitution in an unnoticed and unstructured manner, in the same way that we feel temperature, humidity or the smell of the air, unintentionally and in an embodied manner. Altogether, mood is closer to an embodied haptic sensation than to an external visual percept.

The atmospheric paintings of Joseph Mallord William Turner, the Impressionists and Abstract Expressionists evoke strong sensations of interiority, tactility and the feel of the skin. The art forms of painting, cinema, literature and theatre, and especially music, have been more aware of the significance of atmosphere, feeling and mood than architects. Some time ago I asked a Finnish composer and a pianist[6] about the role of atmospheres in their music. Smiling enigmatically, both answered: 'Music is all atmosphere.' Is this not why music is used in films to create and heighten moods, or to evoke specific tunings and desires in commercial settings? A master novelist's skill as well as that of the film or theatre director is likewise to evoke, articulate and sustain specific moods in order to create the dramatic flow and continuum of the narrative. Should this not also be the task of the architect?

Visual Elementarism and Embodied Understanding

Modernism has favoured an elementarist view where entities are assumed to arise from elementary units and percepts. However, when we study our perceptions and experiences critically, we seem to be perceiving essences of complex multisensory entities such as the characteristics of spaces, places, landscapes and urban settings in an instant. These perceptions take place even quicker than we become conscious of any details, or even our own active attention. We gaze intentionally at visual objects and events, whereas atmospheres come to us omnidirectionally, similarly to acoustic and olfactory sensations. We sense the overall mood, tuning, feeling, ambience and atmosphere of a setting before we have become conscious of it, or have identified any of its constituent features. In the process of design, atmospheric qualities also arise unconsciously in an embodied and haptic manner rather than through conscious retinal strategies and intentions. The sense of a coherent experiential entity is evoked by the designer's sense of existence and body more than conscious and deliberate visual intentionality.

Atmosphere is certainly closely related with the spirit of place, its genius loci, as well as our empathic and affective capacities. In the same way that music can charge a spatial or social situation with a particular mood, the ambience of a landscape, townscape or interior space can project similar integrating and encompassing feelings. Emotional reactions usually arise vaguely, without any distinct focused object or nameable cause. Love, happiness and hate, for instance, are not objects; they are relationships, moods and states of mind. Similarly, we may never intellectually 'understand' a work of art, but it can convey an ineffable influence throughout our entire lives.

'Understanding is not a quality coming to human reality from the outside; it is its characteristic way of existing,' argued Jean-Paul Sartre.[7] This implies that, contrary to our accepted beliefs, we grasp entities before details, singularities before their components, multisensory syntheses before individual sensory features, and emotive or existential meanings before intellectual explanations. We sense embodied and existential meanings outside of the direct, conscious cognitive channels of our life situations. This exemplifies embodied and tacit knowledge. Yet these processes are in evident conflict with established perceptual assumptions as well as the

'Understanding is not a quality coming to human reality from the outside; it is its characteristic way of existing' — Jean-Paul Sartre

Frank Lloyd
Wright, Taliesin
West, Scottsdale,
Arizona,
1938

Perfect harmony and
atmospheric attunement
of landscape and
architecture.

unquestioned priority given to formal and focused vision and cognitive understanding. Since the
Greek philosophers, focused vision has been regarded as synonymous with knowledge and truth.
However, neuroscience lends support to the view that we experience entities before elements,
and we intuit lived meanings without conceptual or verbal signification. Our atmospheric
sense is clearly an evolutionary priority and a consequence of the activities of our right-brain
hemisphere.[8]

Atmospheric Perception in Evolutionary Perspective

I suggest that we have developed our capacities of judging entities at the edge of our awareness
through evolutionary processes. This point is also made by therapist-philosopher Iain
McGilchrist.[9] It has obviously been advantageous for humans to get the meaning of settings
in an instant in terms of their existential and survival qualities. We have developed, as other
animals to various degrees, two independent yet complementary systems of perceiving; one mode
of precise focused perception and the second of diffuse and unfocused peripheral scanning.[10]
Today's science confirms the assumption that we have these two systems of perception – the
conscious and unconscious – and that the first is activated 20 to 30 milliseconds before the latter.
According to scholars such as Anton Ehrenzweig, unconscious scanning is also our creative mode
of perception.[11]

Alvar Aalto,
Säynätsalo Town Hall,
Säynätsalo,
Finland,
1952

An emotive, atmospheric
image of an Italian hill town
concealed in contemporary
architecture.

Peter Zumthor,
Therme Vals,
Graubünden,
Switzerland,
1996

Zumthor is one of the
internationally known
architects today writing
about the significance
of atmospheres in
architecture. His own
architectural works
project a strong
atmospheric quality
and cohesion.

Notes
1. Frank Lloyd Wright, 'The Natural House' [1954], in Bruce Brooks Pfeiffer (ed), *The Essential Frank Lloyd Wright: Critical Writings on Architecture*, Princeton University Press (Princeton, NJ), 2010, p 350.
2. Edward Relph, *Place and Placelessness*, Pion (London), 1986, p 51.
3. For information on proportionality, see: Rudolf Wittkower, *Architectural Principles in the Age of Humanism*, Academy Editions and St Martin's Press (London and New York), 1988; Alberto Pérez-Gómez, *Attunement*, MIT Press (Cambridge, MA and London), 2016; and Juhani Pallasmaa, 'Man, Measure, and Proportion', *Encounters 1 – Juhani Pallasmaa. Architectural Essays*, Rakennustieto Publishing (Helsinki), 2012, pp 231–48.
4. Le Corbusier, *Towards a New Architecture*, The Architectural Press (London), 1959, p 31.
5. The most recent studies of this subject are the books and writings of Peter Zumthor, Tonino Griffero, Jean-Paul Thibault and Alberto Pérez-Gómez.
6. Composer Kalevi Aho and pianist Minna Pöllänen.
7. Jean-Paul Sartre, *The Emotions: An Outline of a Theory*, Carol Publishing Co (New York), 1993, p 9.
8. See Iain McGilchrist, *The Master and His Emissary: The Divided Brain and the Making of the Western World*, Yale University Press (New Haven, CT and London), 2009, p 40.
9. *Ibid*, p 12.
10. *Ibid*, p 102.
11. Anton Ehrenzweig, *The Hidden Order of Art* [1970], Paladin (St Albans), 1973.
12. *Ibid*, p 59.
13. *Ibid*.
14. Iain McGilchrist, 'Tending to the World', in Sarah Robinson and Juhani Pallasmaa (eds), *Mind in Architecture: Neuroscience, Embodiment, and the Future of Design*, MIT Press (Cambridge, MA and London), 2015, pp 99–122.
15. Gabriele d'Annunzio, *Contemplazioni della morte*, Milan, 1912, pp 17–18. As quoted in Gaston Bachelard, *Water and Dreams: An Essay on the Imagination of Matter*, Pegasus Foundation (Dallas, TX), 1983, p 16.
16. Mark Johnson, *The Meaning of the Body: Aesthetics of Human Understanding*, University of Chicago Press (Chicago, IL and London), 2007, p 9.
17. See Ehrenzweig, *op cit*, p 284.
18. Matti Bergström, *Aivojen fysiologiasta ja psyykestä (On the Physiology of the Brain and Psyche)*, WSOY (Helsinki), 1979, pp 77–8.
19. David Howes (ed), *The Sixth Sense Reader*, Berg Publishers (Oxford and New York), 2011, pp 23–4.

However, precision needs to be suppressed for the purpose of observing large entities. The mathematician Jacques Hadamard suggested that even in mathematics, the ultimate decision must be left to the unconscious, as a clear visualisation of problems is usually impossible.[12] He stated categorically that it is mandatory 'to cloud one's consciousness in order to make the right judgement'.[13] McGilchrist relates this divided attention with the differentiation of our two brain hemispheres. It is biologically advantageous to be able to make precise and focused observations and general, vague peripheral ones simultaneously, but would this be impossible within a single system of perception?[14] Focused vision detaches itself from contextual interactions, whereas atmospheric observations fuse and unite all the sensations through the sense of being and self. The omnidirectional senses of hearing, hapticity and smell complement the visual sensations to produce a multisensory existential experience relating us fully with our setting. The experience of atmosphere or mood is thus predominantly an emotive, pre-reflective mode of experience.

Mood and Emotion

> The richest experiences happen long before the soul takes notice. And when we begin to open our eyes to the visible, we have already been supporters of the invisible for a long time.[15]
> — Gabriele d'Annunzio, 1912

One reason why peripheric perceptions have been undervalued, or totally neglected, in architecture is that we have not acknowledged that emotions evaluate, articulate and structure our relations with the world. Emotions are regarded as unconscious, secondary reactions, instead of possessing intentionality and factual value. Yet emotions arise from primal levels of consciousness and, significantly, the first wave of neural signals is always directed to these unconscious systems. As the philosopher Mark Johnson has argued: 'There is no cognition without emotion … emotions are not second-rate cognitions; rather they are affective patterns of our encounter with our world, by which we take the meaning of things at a primordial level.'[16] There is strong evidence that the unconscious system of perception has a higher existential priority.[17] The potential superiority of the unconscious processes in comparison with consciousness is revealed dramatically by the neurological fact that the information-handling capacity of our entire nervous system is estimated to be 10^{15} times the capacity of our conscious system.[18]

The nature of vision itself has been grossly misunderstood as something automatic, objective and precise. Research has revealed that the process of vision is a fragmented and discontinuous mosaic that constantly fuses perceptions with memory and imagination. A visual image itself is composed of separate percepts of colour, form and movement, received at the temporal distance of 40 to 60 milliseconds. In addition, our focused vision sees what we have learned and what we want to see, whereas the peripheral system of perception is capable of identifying what is genuinely new. Mood tunes us emotively with our environment, and as a consequence we do not need to continuously and consciously monitor its overwhelming medley of details.

We are not related to our environments only through the five Aristotelian senses; in fact, *The Sixth Sense Reader* (2011)[19] lists over 30 systems through which we are connected with the world. I suggest that the atmospheric sense could be named our sixth sense, and it is likely to be existentially our most important. Simply, we do not stop at our skin; we extend our bodily self by means of our senses and our technological and constructed extensions. The elecromagnetic waves of the human heart can now be measured from a distance of 5 metres (16 feet) away, but in principle they extend to infinity. Thus, we unknowingly inhabit the entire universe. Δ

CONTRIBUTORS

 ARCHITECTURAL DESIGN

EVOKING THROUGH DESIGN

Alisa Andrasek is director of Biothing and Bloom Games, cofounder of AI-Build, and director of Wonderlab at the Bartlett School of Architecture, University College London (UCL). She holds a professorship at the European Graduate School, and has taught at the Architectural Association Design Research Lab (AA DRL) in London, Columbia Graduate School of Architecture, Planning and Preservation (GSAPP) and Pratt Institute in New York, the University of Pennsylvania (UPenn) in Philadelphia, and RMIT University in Melbourne. She has received numerous awards and her work is in the permanent collections of the Centre Pompidou in Paris, New Museum in New York and FRAC Centre in Orléans.

Isaie Bloch is an architect and the founder of Eragatory, a versatile design practice based in London. His ongoing research and design ambitions focus on the impact of digital craftsmanship within multiple disciplines including architecture, plastic arts, fashion and furniture design. He also lectures at the Bartlett, UCL and University of East London (UEL). Eragatory aims to produce work that embodies crafted digital eclecticism through an engagement with both new digital design processes and old manufacturing techniques, and vice versa. The work of the practice has been published internationally and exhibited widely, including at FRAC, SHOWcabinet in London, and the Experimental Architecture Biennial in Prague.

Benjamin H Bratton is Professor of Visual Arts and Director of the Center for Design and Geopolitics at the University of California, San Diego. His work spans philosophy, art, design and computer science. He is also a Professor of Digital Design at the European Graduate School and Visiting Faculty at the Southern California Institute of Architecture (SCI-Arc) in Los Angeles. Recent books include *The Stack: On Software and Sovereignty* (MIT Press, 2016).

Mario Carpo is Reyner Banham Professor of Architectural Theory and History at the Bartlett, UCL. His research and publications focus on the relationship between architectural theory, cultural history, and the history of media and information technology. His *Architecture in the Age of Printing* (MIT Press, 2001) has been translated into several languages. His most recent books are *The Alphabet and the Algorithm* (MIT Press, 2011), a history of digital design theory; and *The Digital Turn in Architecture, 1992–2012* (John Wiley & Sons, 2013).

Marjan Colletti is an architect, educator, researcher and author. He is Full Professor in Architecture and Post Digital Practice and Director of Computing at the Bartlett, UCL; Chair Professor of Building Design and Construction, Founder of REX|LAB and Head of the Institute of Experimental Architecture at the University of Innsbruck; and cofounder and co-principal of MAM-arch in London. He has published various books on design research and research-led education in architecture, including *Exuberance: New Virtuosity in Contemporary Architecture* (2010), and *Digital Poetics: An Open Theory of Design-Research in Architecture* (Routledge, 2013). He also lectures, exhibits and publishes internationally.

Mark Foster Gage is the founder of Mark Foster Gage Architects in New York City, as well as the Assistant Dean of the Yale School of Architecture in New Haven, Connecticut. His pioneering work has been exhibited in institutions including the Museum of Modern Art (MoMA) in New York and the Museum of the Art Institute of Chicago, and featured, among others, in *Vogue*, *Fast Company*, *Harper's Bazaar* and the *New York Times*. He has written extensively on design and aesthetics in academic publications including *Δ*, *Volume*, *Fulcrum*, *Perspecta* and *LOG*, for which he also guest co-edited issue #19.

Eric Goldemberg is the co-founder of MONAD Studio, a design research practice with a focus on spatial perception related to rhythmic affect. He is Associate Professor and Digital Design Coordinator at Florida International University in Miami, and the author of the book *Pulsation in Architecture* (J Ross Publishing, 2011), which highlights the range and complexity of sensations involved in constructing rhythmic ensembles. His work has been widely published, including in the *New York Times*, *The Guardian*, *Forbes Magazine* and *Architectural Record*.

Camille Lacadée is a cofounder of New-Territories/M4 and R&Sie(n) with François Roche. She graduated in 2009 from the École Spéciale d'Architecture in Paris, after passing her RIBA Part 1 in 2008 at the AA in London.

Michael Loverich was born on an island in the moist forests near Seattle. He graduated from the University of California, Los Angeles (UCLA) with a Master's in Architecture before working at Reiser + Umemoto and Snøhetta. In 2008 he cofounded The Bittertang Farm, a new type of architectural firm centred on human pleasure, frothiness and neotenous forms. He has built numerous projects including a waxy environment, a pregnant piñata and various inflatable pavilions. He currently teaches at UPenn.

John McMorrough is a founding partner of studioAPT (Architecture Project Theory). His work is motivated by the conviction that architecture, as a field of knowledge, continually needs to situate its productive and projective capacities, in both the reconsideration of its conceptual legacies and the testing of its competencies vis-à-vis the specifics of building. He has worked for design offices in Kansas City, New York, Boston and Rotterdam, and has taught architectural theory and design at Yale University, the Ohio State University in Columbus, and the University of Applied Arts in Vienna. He is currently an associate professor of architecture at the University of Michigan in Ann Arbor.

Juhani Pallasmaa, architect and professor emeritus, has worked in urban, architectural, exhibition, product and graphic design, in collaboration with other architects and through his own office (1983–2012). He has held several positions, including Professor and Dean at the Helsinki University of Technology, Director of the Museum of Finnish Architecture, and Rector of the Institute of Industrial Arts, Helsinki. He has been a visiting professor in several notable universities in the US, and lectured around the world. He has published 45 books, and received several Finnish and international prizes and honours for architecture and criticism. From 2008 to 2014 he was a member of the Pritzker Architecture Prize Jury. His widely known books include *The Eyes of the Skin: Architecture and the Senses* (1996) and *The Thinking Hand* (2009), both published by John Wiley & Sons.

Jason Payne is the Principal of Hirsuta and Associate Professor of Architecture at UCLA. He has also taught at UPenn, SCI-Arc, Pratt Institute, Polis University in Tirana, Albania, Rice University in Texas, Bennington College in Vermont, and Rensselaer Polytechnic Institute in New York. In his early career he worked as a project designer for Studio Libeskind and Reiser + Umemoto, later cofounding the award-winning office Gnuform, best known for the NGTV© Bar (2006 AIA Design Award) and the 2006 PS1/MoMA Young Architects Program entry Purple Haze. Through Hirsuta he continues to produce works informed by intensive research and an experimental approach.

Wolf D Prix is the Design Principal and CEO of Coop Himmelb(l)au. He studied architecture at the Vienna University of Technology and the AA, as well as at SCI-Arc. He is the Design Principal of the European Central Bank (ECB) in Frankfurt, BMW Welt in Munich, Musée des Confluences in Lyon, Dalian International Conference Center in China, and the Museum of Contemporary Art and Planning Exhibition (MOCAPE) in Shenzhen. He has received numerous awards including the Great Austrian State Award and the Austrian Decoration of Honour for Science and Art, the Erich-Schelling-Architecture Prize and the Hessian Cultural Prize.

Gilles Retsin is the founder of Gilles Retsin Architecture, a young award-winning architecture and design practice based in London that investigates new architectural models that engage with the potential of increased computational power and fabrication to generate buildings and objects with a previously unseen structure, detail and materiality. He graduated from the AA DRL, is a senior lecturer at UEL, and alongside his practice directs a research cluster at the Bartlett, UCL, exploring robotic manufacturing and large-scale 3D printing.

François Roche is the principal of New-Territories/M4, currently based in Bangkok, cofounder and principal of R&Sie(n) in Paris, and a guest research professor at several universities. New-Territories/M4 is a studio of contingent scenarios, seeking to articulate the real and/or fictional, the geographic situations and narrative structures that can transform them, with technology, robotic and human natures, both physiological and psychological.

Roland Snooks is the director of the architecture practice Studio Roland Snooks, and of research lab Kokkugia. He is a senior lecturer at RMIT University having previously taught widely in the US, including at UPenn, SCI-Arc, Pratt Institute, and Columbia University in New York. He received a PhD from RMIT University, focused on behavioural processes of formation that draw from the logic of swarm intelligence. He holds a Master's in advanced architectural design from Columbia. He also directs the Architectural Robotics Lab at RMIT.

Andrew Saunders is an Associate Professor of Architecture at the University of Pennsylvania School of Design, and founding principal of Andrew Saunders Architecture + Design, which is committed to the tailoring of innovative digital methodologies to provoke novel exchange and reassessment of the broader cultural context. He received his Bachelor of Architecture from the University of Arkansas, and a Master's in Architecture with Distinction from the Harvard University Graduate School of Design (GSD). He has taught and guest lectured at various institutions, including Cooper Union in New York and the Cranbrook Academy of Art in Michigan, and most recently was Assistant Professor of Architecture and Head of Graduate Studies at Rensselaer Polytechnic Institute.

Michael Young is an architect and educator practising in New York City where he is a founding partner of the architectural design studio Young & Ayata. He is an Assistant Professor at Cooper Union, and has previously taught design studios and seminars at Yale, Princeton, Columbia, Syracuse, Pratt Institute and the University of Innsbruck. His work has been exhibited internationally. Young & Ayata recently received a first-place prize to design the Bauhaus Museum in Dessau, Germany, and were recipients of the 2014 Young Architects Prize from the Architectural League of New York.

What is Architectural Design?

Founded in 1930, *Architectural Design* (△) is an influential and prestigious publication. It combines the currency and topicality of a newsstand journal with the rigour and production qualities of a book. With an almost unrivalled reputation worldwide, it is consistently at the forefront of cultural thought and design.

Each title of △ is edited by an invited Guest-Editor, who is an international expert in the field. Renowned for being at the leading edge of design and new technologies, △ also covers themes as diverse as architectural history, the environment, interior design, landscape architecture and urban design.

Provocative and inspirational, △ inspires theoretical, creative and technological advances. It questions the outcome of technical innovations as well as the far-reaching social, cultural and environmental challenges that present themselves today.

For further information on △, subscriptions and purchasing single issues see:

www.architectural-design-magazine.com

Volume 85 No 6
ISBN 978 1118 915646

Volume 86 No 1
ISBN 978 1118 910641

Volume 86 No 2
ISBN 978 1118 736166

Volume 86 No 3
ISBN 978 1118 972465

Volume 86 No 4
ISBN 978 1118 951057

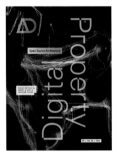

Volume 86 No 5
ISBN 978 1118 954980